**Architectural Design**
November/December 2007

# Made in Ind

Guest-edited by
Kazi K Ashraf

C000113319

wiley.com

ISBN-978 0470 03476 7
Profile No 190
Vol 77 No 6

Editorial Offices
International House
Ealing Broadway Centre
London W5 5DB

T: +44 (0)20 8326 3800
F: +44 (0)20 8326 3801
E: architecturaldesign@wiley.co.uk

Editor
Helen Castle

Production Editor
Elizabeth Gongde

Project Management
Caroline Ellerby

Design and Prepress
Artmedia Press, London

Printed in Italy by Conti Tipocolor

Advertisement Sales
Faith Pidduck/Wayne Frost
T: +44 (0)1243 770254
E: fpidduck@wiley.co.uk

Editorial Board
Will Alsop, Denise Bratton, Mark Burry, André
Chaszar, Nigel Coates, Peter Cook, Teddy Cruz,
Max Fordham, Massimiliano Fuksas, Edwin
Heathcote, Michael Hensel, Anthony Hunt,
Charles Jencks, Jan Kaplicky, Robert Maxwell,
Jayne Merkel, Michael Rotondi, Leon van Schaik,
Neil Spiller, Michael Weinstock, Ken Yeang

Contributing Editors
Jeremy Melvin
Jayne Merkel

All Rights Reserved. No part of this publication
may be reproduced, stored in a retrieval system
or transmitted in any form or by any means,
electronic, mechanical, photocopying, recording,
scanning or otherwise, except under the terms
of the Copyright, Designs and Patents Act 1988
or under the terms of a licence issued by the
Copyright Licensing Agency Ltd, 90 Tottenham
Court Road, London W1T 4LP, UK, without the
permission in writing of the Publisher.

Front cover: Rahul Mehrotra, House on an
Orchard, near Ahmedabad, 2004. © RMA, photo
Rajesh Vora

Requests to the Publisher should be addressed to:
Permissions Department,
John Wiley & Sons Ltd,
The Atrium
Southern Gate
Chichester,
West Sussex PO19 8SQ
England

F: +44 (0)1243 770571
E: permreq@wiley.co.uk

Subscription Offices UK
John Wiley & Sons Ltd
Journals Administration Department
1 Oldlands Way, Bognor Regis
West Sussex, PO22 9SA
T: +44 (0)1243 843272
F: +44 (0)1243 843232
E: cs-journals@wiley.co.uk

[ISSN: 0003-8504]

AD is published bimonthly and is available to
purchase on both a subscription basis and as
individual volumes at the following prices.

Single Issues
Single issues UK: £22.99
Single issues outside UK: US$45.00
Details of postage and packing charges
available on request.

Annual Subscription Rates 2007
Institutional Rate
Print only or Online only: UK£175/US$315
Combined Print and Online: UK£193/US$347
Personal Rate
Print only: UK£110/US$170
Student Rate
Print only: UK£70/US$110
Prices are for six issues and include postage
and handling charges. Periodicals postage paid
at Jamaica, NY 11431. Air freight and mailing in
the USA by Publications Expediting Services
Inc, 200 Meacham Avenue, Elmont, NY 11003
Individual rate subscriptions must be paid by
personal cheque or credit card. Individual rate
subscriptions may not be resold or used as
library copies.

All prices are subject to change
without notice.

Postmaster
Send address changes to 3 Publications
Expediting Services, 200 Meacham Avenue,
Elmont, NY 11003

# C O N T E N T S

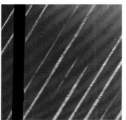

# Editorial

*'A fairground of monsters and miracles, India-town is different from other boomtowns. Don't be fooled by the plethora of cranes and confuse it with China.'*

Ramesh Biswas, 'One Space, Many Worlds', p 25

The current economic excitement over the Chino-India region has meant that India's development has in recent years been all too readily identified with that of China. The figures produced by analysts to describe the 'Chindia effect' reflect this buzz; it has been projected that if the current growth persists in China and India, by 2050 the two nations will account for roughly half of global output. Encompassing a third of the world's population, this greater Asian region has the potential of not only huge domestic markets, but also cheap, highly skilled labour and governments that pursue capital-friendly policies. The impact of this will be to effectively position the world at a tipping point in terms of economic and political power. When the full realisation grew over India's potency as an economic powerhouse, both as a nation and in the greater context of Southeast Asia, two or three years ago, like any other editor my antennae were out. My motivations for wanting to commission an issue of *AD* dedicated to the subject were admittedly, in the first instance, simplistic. I was in no doubt that the confluence of a booming economy, globalisation and a rich cultural tradition – both historic and modern – rendered it fertile territory. The potential of a publication that could deal with contemporary architecture with acumen and insight – beyond the current treatments of China – only transpired when I saw Kazi Ashraf present the subject of current Indian culture and transnationalism at the Architectural League in New York for the launch of Sara Caples' and Everardo Jefferson's issue *The New Mix: Culturally Dynamic Architecture*, for which Ashraf was a contributor.

Ashraf has configured an issue that is able to deal with all the complexities and contradictions of India and the greater subcontinent: a region that is experiencing unprecedented prosperity, while much of its population remains stuck in a cycle of destitute poverty; it is an uneven urban landscape of decay and opulence, slum dwelling and emerging middle-class townships of pastiche mansions. While the majority of the population are embracing new technologies with alacrity, the new media is also effectively heightening anxiety and awakening superstitious beliefs; as a nation, India has for the past 60 years often been defining itself through its break with its colonial past, but with globalisation could, in Sunil Khilnani's words, be in danger of losing its 'self-understanding' in terms of its culture and architecture. According to Ashraf, India is a nation of 'messy cities', 'transmogrificatiton' and 'blanketing landscapes'. Through a set of fascinating critical essays, Ashraf and his contributors adeptly define the many layers and simultaneous developments of a nation and its greater region. Threaded through this in *contraposto* is the work of some 25 architectural practices who are designing buildings for India from at home and abroad. Diverse in approach, style, type and context, they are in a sense the material evidence of the shifting, multilayered landscape of India in the present and the future. ⌂

Helen Castle

**Rahul Mehrotra Associates, Rural Campus for Tata Institute of Social Sciences (TISS), Tuljapur, Maharashtra, 2004**
Maintaining a small practice in Mumbai, while also teaching internationally, Mehrotra focuses on culturally specific design solutions, such as this one for a rural campus that is clustered around internal courtyards. These sheltered spaces respond to the local climate while also encouraging social interaction between students.

Text © 2007 John Wiley & Sons Ltd. Image © RMA, photo Rajesh Vora

# Raga India
## Architecture in the Time of Euphoria

As India celebrates the 60th anniversary of its independence, guest-editor **Kazi K Ashraf** introduces this special title of *AD* by holding up a barometer to the nation's cultural identity. Can architecture be best understood through a local sense of place or globalisation? What are the driving impulses behind India's chaotic urban landscape that is simultaneously 'messy' and utopian? Can Indian culture be best understood as a national entity or through a more elusive subcontinental substance?

## The Pickle Factory

In a setting of an allegorical pickle factory – the pickle or chutney is a virulent Postmodern trope and decisively Indian – Saleem Sinai churns another story of national and autobiographical destiny in Salman Rushdie's *Midnight's Children*. Rushdie's alter ego both refigures the present and prefigures the upcoming India in clairvoyant pickle jars. There are 30 bottles on the factory shelf. Twenty-nine bottles are full, and each one makes up each chapter/episode of the tumultuous and fabulous history of India after its independence in 1947. The thirtieth bottle is empty, waiting to be filled and written in. What will the next vessel contain?

## Vritra's Ghost

The Husain-Doshi Gufa in Ahmedabad, which houses the work of the irrepressible artist MF Husain, was built in 1994 as a collaborative project between the artist and the architect Balkrishna Doshi. The undulating structure of the Gufa, dug cave-like into the earth, blurring the edge of building and landscape, has the unmistakable physiognomy of a terrestrial creature with its vertebras, ligaments and eyes (Husain also painted a black serpent on the wall). The Gufa is also Doshi's counter-homage to Corbusier's paean to the right-angle. With every square foot, including the floor and columns, warping every other way and without a horizontal plane of repose, the Gufa is a perceptual *tour de force*. It marks a departure from the rational, technocratic modality represented by crystalline and cubic forms, upraised in the sun, towards reviving suppressed depths of the unconscious, as it were.

Vritra lay very dead, and not unlike Vastupurusa upon whose dismembered body a new episode and edifice might rise.[1] Vritra, a terrestrial dragon, held on to the waters of the world, as the story goes, until the celestial and luminous Indra ('smasher of enclosures') arrived to destroy the 99 fortresses of Vritra, kill the dragon, and release imprisoned rivers. On the destroyed ramparts and ligaments of a telluric structure arose a brave, new world. And in Ahmedabad, in a resurrected moment, a contrapuntal architecture arises uncannily from the ground, coinciding with India's increasing embrace of the fabulous and metarational.

## From Raga to Ragas

*August in Bombay: a month of festivals, the month of Krishna's birthday and Coconut Day; and this year – fourteen hours to go, thirteen, twelve – there was an extra festival on the calendar, a new myth to celebrate, because a nation which had never previously existed was about to win its freedom, catapulting us into a world which, although it had five thousand years of history, although it had invented the game of chess and traded with Middle Kingdom Egypt, was nevertheless quite imaginary; into a mythical land, a country which would never exist except by the efforts of a phenomenal*

**Balkrishna Doshi, Husain-Doshi Gufa, Ahmedabad, 1994**
Terrestrial architecture and fabulous mythologies.

*collective will – except in a dream we all agreed to dream; it was a mass fantasy shared in varying degrees by Bengali and Punjabi, Madrasi and Jat, and would periodically need the sanctification and renewal which can only be provided by rituals of blood. India, the new myth – a collective fiction in which anything was possible, a fable rivaled only by two other mighty fantasies: money and God.*

— Salman Rushdie, *Midnight's Children*, 1980[2]

The pan-Indian edifice for whose mythical soul a French-Swiss architect wrote an urban epic at the foothills of the Himalayas, and which ironically has now been usurped by a (Hindu) religious right, exhibits multiple fissures. The tryst with destiny, as Nehru scheduled, gives way to a hundred trysts and a million destinies. Architects now hesitate to talk of *an* Indian value as debates rage between essentialist and differentiated positions. While a quasi-nationalist articulation

**Surendran Nair, *Auto da fe*, 1996**
'It's what you oughtn't to do but you do anyway.' The painting is part of Nair's 'Collected Mythologies', a body of work about belonging and dissent.

The road to Gurgaon: the city in search of urbanism.

was premised in most work until the late 1980s, architects, like Prem Chandavarkar in his essay in this issue of *AD*, currently consider the palpability and specificity of places in lieu of a singular spatiality of the nation. A critical post-nationalist practice now maintains a triple resistance – to both Indianism and globalism – and at the same time does not appear to be 'backward'.

### Sundarnagar – A Place Called Elsewhere
Urbanism is the Achilles heel in the rush for euphoria. An upsurge of houses, malls, IT campuses and condominiums marks the architectural landscape in market-driven India, yet there is little attention to how the individual creations come together as a social and spatial matrix among themselves and with the existent. In his essay Ramesh Biswas writes that a paradigmatic thinking in city-making is needed for this unprecedented urban phenomenon, notwithstanding forms of media, broadcast and cinematic urbanism. The urban utopia of Chandigarh that was criticised for its alienating features has been superseded by a greater phantasmagoria – of a Gurgaon in Delhi or Hirandani in Mumbai, which are at best exclusive places in relation to the larger context, or, more questionably, in Gayatri Spivak's rephrasing of global capital behaviour, 'secessionist'.[3]

Popular Hindi films provide a vicarious view of this new translocation. The setting of the 2003 film *Mein Prem Ki Diwani Hoon* is a fictional town called Sundarnagar, or 'the city beautiful'. It is a place of bourgeois opulence, of resplendent houses populated by patriarchs and purveyors of tradition. The lawns to the houses are wide, and the driveways regal, while the riot-free, languorous town harbours manicured parks (obviously water supply is not a problem), quaint telephone booths (no sign of the ubiquitous ISD-NSW-Local),

and lush outdoor spaces for cavorting (no pulsating mob either). In the film, Sundarnagar is depicted as a town in India, but the reality is that the entire film was shot in New Zealand. The Indian city of Sundarnagar may be fictive, but it is depicted in a real place, and that place is elsewhere, and that is the fixation in the Hindi filmic imagination: the relentless flight towards elsewhere.

This flight is embedded and encoded in multiple realms, from the 'song-site' numbers in Bollywood filmic productions to new building configurations.[4] This presents a juxtaposition of the place here and now and a place elsewhere, the messy city and a dream topography, where the former is of a native and the latter of a transnational provenance. The places from elsewhere in the song-sites, which are real and actual, become fictive in the Hindi film narrative because the places are not named, nor located with precision; they are literally framed to be 'foreign', to be elsewhere. What makes *Mein Prem Ki Diwani Hoon* striking is that it takes the elsewhere of the song-site to the entire film. The longing for elsewhere – or the desire to secede – is increasingly being embodied in new building configurations that are radically altering the urban landscape.

Despite the exhilarating lightness of arbitrariness, the relentless dissolution of geography and the adoption of mimicry as an economic policy (Meenakshi in Mangalore presenting herself as Monica to a housewife in Minneapolis), many architects return to the intractable and redemptive theme of place specificities. The critical question – whether it is in this issue for Bijoy Jain in the humid swamps of Mumbai, Prem Chandavarkar in a temperate and verdant Bangalore, or Rafiq Azam in the terracotta terrain of Dhaka – is still 'where is architecture' and not so much 'what is architecture'.

### House Works
Housing is out, houses are in. If one allows for some more divine apparitions, gods are now in small structures, and in their meticulous crafting, where the condensed poetics and

The new battleground.

**Hafeez Contractor, Proposed Software Development Centre, 2005**
Fabulous forms and phantasmagoric visions.

tectonics negotiate the pendulum of the inevitable here-ness and the tantalising elsewhere. Since the 1960s, housing (and other public projects) was a major domain of the Indian architectural enterprise that reflected a communitarian concern of the post-Corbusian/Nehruvian period. The emerging economy and radical shift in the lives of the middle classes have now opened up new desires for articulating the house. The Turkish novelist Orhan Pamuk writes that the way to understand the people who have been part of the astounding expansion of the middle classes of India and China is to see their private lives reflected in novels.[5] In India, a vast part of that transformational imaginary is being narrated through the house, from opulent *havelis* (private residences) and fictive 'farmhouses', to the elegant constructions of Bijoy Jain, Rahul Mehrotra and others, and the delectably delirious propositions of Michael Sorkin.

The dialogical continuum of house/home with the world is being refashioned according to the emergent 'secessionist' tendency to Home versus World. It is also in the context where the public building recedes in the social horizon, on the one hand, and unprecedented atomisation proliferates socially on the other, that house/home is now a major site of the architectural exegesis in India. Whether it is merely another object in the consumerist cosmos (KK Birla of the famous industrialist family points out that what was once a symbol of attainment, the brick house, shifted first to the motor scooter and now to the car),[6] and whether it retains the gravitas of dwelling, remains unclear, but the projects presented in this issue return to the house as an embodiment of situation and materiality.

## Reincarnating Types

Rahul Mehrotra's Orchard House outside Ahmedabad recalls both the courtyard paradigm of hot-dry climates and a reactive interiority that may stem from the raucous urbanism of Indian cities (Mehrotra explains that his architectural vocabulary hinges on the reading of his city of practice, Mumbai). While courtyard houses are by nature exclusionary (socially and visually), the redemption is in the itinerary, in the arrival and passage through the various articulated thresholds articulated by walls into the ecstatic focus of the house: the open-to-sky court.

The obverse of that model is the pavilion where the inner court gives way to a canopy, and the predominantly solid wall dematerialises into perforations, membranes, lattices and *jails* (perforated screens). Much of the architecture of Bijoy Jain (Studio Mumbai Architects) is a delightful celebration of the pavilion, approximating the Sri Lankan architect Geoffrey Bawa's consideration of the house-as-a-garden in the hot-humid milieu. Whether in tactile-rich wooden slats, or a diaphanous luminous screen, Jain's architecture amplifies the phenomenal and spatial continuum between the house and landscape in a moisture-saturated environment. However, such singular typologies are not always possible as one confronts inevitable complexities, either programmatic or urban. Samira Rathod, in her Mariwala House, creates a horizontal symphony of disparate pieces that are tactile, colourful and voluble. Mathew & Ghosh, for their studio and residence on a small site in Bangalore, produce a compacted bricolage of diverse pieces as an urban essay. In their attempt to reconfigure the contemporary urban box, in a context

**Sanjay Puri Architects, Silver jewellery mall and office tower, Vashi, Mumbai, 2008**
A spectacular presence.

where a purity or unity is no longer possible, the architectural body is composed of fragmentations and a patchwork of memories and events. Rafiq Azam, in Dhaka, rearranges the conventional location of building, garden and landscape, and in doing so boldly devises a house of landscape layers even within the city. Many of these works share a material and expressive language with a trans-Asian tropical modernity.

A transformation is also happening where architects fear to tread – rural houses or dwellings for the economically disadvantaged, both of which constitute a significant figure in South Asia. For his contribution to this issue of *AD*, Adnan Morshed, in a sort of subaltern narrative, traces the anthropological metamorphosis of rural dwellings touched by the Grameen Bank housing programme, and argues that a quiet revolution is happening to these 'timeless' villages, something that needs to be incorporated into the story of Indian and South Asian architecture, especially as the axis of contention in the new economy is increasingly between the city and village.

## Gandhi in Exile

*Our strategy should be not only to confront empire, but to lay siege to it. To deprive it of oxygen. To shame it. To mock it. With our art, our music, our literature, our stubbornness, our joy, our brilliance, our sheer relentlessness – and our ability to tell our own stories. Stories that are different from the ones we're being brainwashed to believe.*
— Arundhati Roy, 2003[7]

Our architecture? I was not wholly surprised on a visit a year ago to see Gandhi's ashram in Wardha (Nagpur) rather desolate like a residue of an abandoned village. A few Japanese tourists sat down for a lesson in the *charka* (spinning wheel), while giggling couples from the neighbouring areas roamed the yards in oblivious frivolity. If the *charka* is an emblem of sustainability – and Gandhi is to be credited for that much fashionable architectural term now – it is now as alien as Buddha's *dharma-chakra* (the wheel of law). I was more surprised to find the name of the venerable Ivan Illich on a

dusty, monotyped pamphlet on Gandhi's house. Written in 1978, as an ethical and sociological explanation of the emblematic *bapukuti* (Gandhi's own house in the ashram), the pamphlet predicted the challenges of the coming decades, the onrush of accumulation and consumption in a 'shining and incredible' India. Both Nehru and Gandhi represented Modernist self-reflectivity, but while Nehru professed what was then an internationalist position, Gandhi appeared parochially nationalist. The matter has reversed now. If Nehru is the Modernist of the now much discredited industrial-socialist makeover, Gandhi's experiments with himself align with the radical Modernist project of transfiguration: through the ascetic body in the minimalist space. I see Gandhi sitting on the floor of the Farnsworth House, and being quite at home behind the large plate-glass walls. The once national is now the irrefutable international, but in his own ashram he is ironically absent.

Following Illich's prognosis, an accelerated consumerism proceeds at warp speed (pun intended) throwing caution to the wind and revelling in a febrile architectural outpour India has never seen. What to make of this all?

**Studio Mumbai Architects, Jamshyd Sethna House, Mumbai, 2007**
The landscape and an architecture of the pavilion.

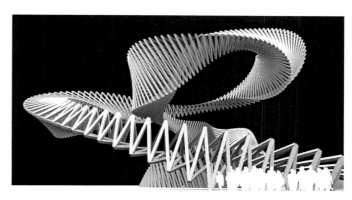

**Nuru Karim, 'Charkha': Celebrating Mahatma Gandhi's Philosophy of the Spinning Wheel, Pune, India, projected 2008**
Spinning the Wheel competition-winning entry for an Architectural Symbol for Contemporary India.

**Samira Rathod, My House, Alibag, Maharashtra, 2005**
Weathering the house: an artificial sheath of rain that can be turned on to create a cooler microclimate.

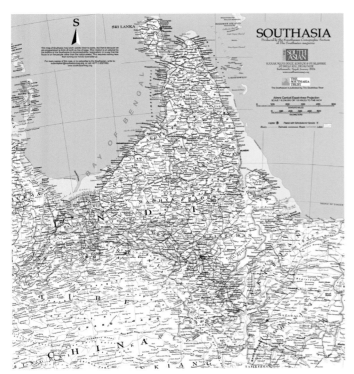

Looking at the subcontinent: a Himalayan view.

## Anthologising India

India is a giant squid that every now and then must be wrestled to the ground in order to make sense of it. And in the melee, one tentacle does not know what the others are doing. Is India poised for an economic lift-off the likes of which has not been witnessed before, or is it perched on the precipice of an urban and ecological cataclysm? Is India about the irrefutable phantasmagoria of Bollywood or the timeless poise of a Bharatnatyam? Is the Indian an argumentative one or a meditative one? Is India about the conciliatory Gufa of Doshi and Husain, or the virulence of the religious activists who vandalised it?[8] Is India in the end really about India itself, as understood by notions of nations, or the much more fluid, elusive and yet definitive subcontinental substance? When the

giant squid is finally pinned to the ground, all tentacles flailing, one realises it is not a multitentacled squid after all, but a hydra-headed creature.

With the task of mapping contemporary architecture, I wanted to see what analogy could be drawn from literary anthologies. Among various anthologies of the vibrant literary outpouring of India,[9] that edited by Adil Jussawalla, a very early collection (1974), is particularly prescient. Jussawalla opens the volume with an excerpt from Qurratulain Hyder's reflection on statelessness from her transhistorical fiction *The River of Fire*.[10] While a Himalayan view of India is always a dubious project, Hyder's *River* speaks of the 'Indian' state of mind that overflows the imperviousness of new nation-states. Within an effluent history, it charts the cultural fluidity, geographic porosity and transnational mobility that describe the South Asian meta-national matrix.

Is the vitality in literature matched in architecture? As this issue will show, there is certainly a definitive inauguration of new latitudes and energies in Indian and subcontinental architecture. The enigmatic empty jar of Saleem/Salman that portended an archaeology of the future is now and here. And if that bottle were filled, would it look like the present issue of *AD*, a raga of indelible vitality? Δ

### Notes

1. In an idea where ritualised death is conflated with the production of the mandala, Vastupurusa is an undefined being who was seized by the gods and pinned down to the earth, and whose dismembered body was distributed across the gridded mandala before building and habitation could begin. Vritra is mentioned in ancient Vedic texts as a terrestrial creature who controls the waters and must be annihilated – in this case by the celestial Indra – before a proper socialised beginning. Both myths perhaps circulate the prehistoric subjugation of terrestrial and locational symbolism by the predominantly celestial and abstract Vedic ideology.
2. Salman Rushdie, *Midnight's Children*, Penguin Group (New York), 1980.
3. Gayatri Chakravorty Spivak, 'City, Country, Agency', presented at the conference 'Theatres of Decolonization', Chandigarh, 1995. Spivak was referring to a statement on the nature of electronic capitalism by the US Secretary of Labor.
4. The 'song-site' is a literal space of the exotic and faraway in popular Indian filmic imagination that weaves music, dance, couture, urban and landscape imagery into a phantasmagoria of dreams and desires.
5. Orhan Pamuk in an interview with Alexander Star in *The New York Times*, 15 August 2004.
6. Dr KK Birla, 'India 2020', *Hindustan Times*, 9 May 2007.
7. Arundhati Roy, from her address at the 2003 World Social Forum, Porto Allegre, Brazil.
8. Bajrang Dal activists vandalised the Gufa in 1998 over MF Husain's artwork in what appears to continue up to now as the Hindu religious right's policing of art and cultural production.
9. I especially mention Salman Rushdie, *Mirrorwork*: *Fifty Years of Indian Writing*, Vintage (London), 1997; Amit Chaudhuri, *Picador Book of Modern Indian Literature*, Picador (London), 2001; and *The Granta Book of India*, London and New York, 2004.
10. Adil J Jussawalla, *New Writings in India*, Penguin (Harmondsworth), 1974. Qurratulain Hyder's *River of Fire* was first published as *Aag Ka Dariya* in 1957.

Text © 2007 John Wiley & Sons Ltd. Images: p 6 © Surendran Nair, photo Himanshu Pahad; p 7 © Vastu Shilpa Consultants, photo John Panifer; p 8(t) © Kazi Ashraf; p 8(b) © Mayank Bhatnagar, www.graphicreflections.org; p 9 © Architect Hafeez Contractor; p 10(t) © Sanjay Puri Architects; p 10(c) © Courtesy of Studio Mumbai Architects; p 10(b) © Nuru B Karim; p 11(t) © SRDA, photo David D'Souza; p 11(b) HIMAL SOUTHASIAN, www.himalmag.com

# The India Project

While pockets of India are now approaching the living standards of
Switzerland, other regions are debilitated by a level of poverty that is akin to
that of Zimbabwe. **Sunil Khilnani** asks what remains of the universalist
project of India's political founders. Has architecture, in the rush for market
and economic success, lost its self-understanding?

A landscape of frenetic changes.

The realm of private capital: self-generated, controlled and insulated.

The Indian economy is shuddering into life with extraordinarily visible as well as variable effects: parts of India's vast landscape are being roiled in turbulent wind tunnels of frenetic change, others are trapped in still, doldrum air. In the richest parts of the country – the three states of Punjab, Haryana and Maharashtra (whose populations at respectively 24, 21 and 96 million add up to around 140 million Indians) – people enjoy per capita incomes three and a half times or more, and have ten times as many vehicles, as their poorest compatriots in the states of Bihar, Uttar Pradesh and Madhya Pradesh (whose combined population is 300 million). If such patterns of uneven growth continue, in coming decades the Indian Union will increasingly resemble one of those 'exquisite corpses' children like to draw – disparate bits, dreamed up by different imaginations and endowed with quite different abilities, whose principle of connection will be hard to discern or justify. As some commentators have pointed out, it will be a country in which parts will approach the living standards of Switzerland, while others will be like Zimbabwe.

Can one, in such a territory of fragmented success, speak of a common political project, let alone a continuous architectural imagination which might express and help to constitute this? And why should one even try?

What is striking about India's upswing – wherever it is happening – is its indifference to politics: markets continue to boom, regardless of terrorist attacks, venal politicians and a regional neighbourhood of profound instability. In a little triumph of the theory of capital, the economic seems to have insulated itself from the political, just as the successful in India have seceded from the unsuccessful, retreating to their walled gardens and apartment buildings.

It is this economic success, abstracted from political context, that Indian elites today seek to project. It has caught the attention of the world – and has even come to be seen by the West as threatening. There is an easy, universal comprehensibility about economic success and failure – its measurement is standard and has a global currency. Yet what is distinctive to India has been, and still is, its political ambition and achievement: the creation, out of material unparalleled both in its diversity and its entrenched hierarchy, of an open society committed to democratic politics, to a pluralism of human life, and to a project of common development. This was the founding idea of India, the unlikely project that men like Nehru embarked the country on at the midpoint of the 20th century.

One must recall some of the most radical aspects of this idea of India, sometimes forgotten in an age when our options seem to have narrowed either to an acceptance of homogenising globalisation, or to a violent rejection of this. Although this vision of India emerged out of, and was shaped by, its antagonistic relationship to colonial power, it never sought refuge in safe harbours of nativism, in a culturalist rejection of the colonial inheritance. It was a profoundly universalist project, an alternative universalism based not on a deluded sense of Indian self-sufficiency, but one which was ready to argue with the West, as well as with itself. It was prepared to deploy critical reason, in deciding what to adopt

Nehru's project of alternative universalism: 'It hits you on the head and makes you think.' Le Corbusier's Assembly Building, Chandigarh, 1963.

and to dispense with from both its own traditions and from the West. It was, as articulated by men like Nehru, a critical Modernism, distinctive in its ambition to structure diversity into a common national project seeing, in defiance of classical Western theories of nationalism, diversity as a source of strength rather than weakness.

It was distinctive, too, in the forms of activist resistance through which India projected itself in the world. India took a position between the powerful and the powerless, the rich and the poor, and between contending ideological groups, the West and the socialist world. It sought autonomy in the international domain by refusing to participate in alignments, in treaties and in markets, all of which it viewed as skewed in favour of the more powerful. This was an extension into the international domain of the Gandhian strategy of boycotts and fasts. As Nehru put it in the mid-1950s: 'Asian strength exists in the negative sense of resisting.'[1] This resistance was double in its senses: a resistance to the sirens of global power, but equally a resistance to the pulls of narrow and exclusive definitions of culture and tradition.

This founding project, based on India's diversity, its desire to find its own terms on which to engage with the world, and on a belief in a benevolent state, was given form in policies, institutions and choices. But it also elaborated itself in a rhetoric of performance. From the carefully calibrated cabinet ministries (making sure they included some members from each of the country's minorities and regions), to such events as the well-orchestrated 26 January Republic Day parades (when a well-marshalled microcosm of the country processed down Lutyens' spinal boulevard), and the creation of industrial towns, and from steel plants like Bhilai (designed as melting pots of caste hierarchy and religious difference where the new secular, productive, Indian citizen would be created), onwards to Nehru's commissioning of Le Corbusier to build Chandigarh: such ploys and ventures expressed a will to create a public realm through a kind of architecture of emblems that would represent Indian autonomy as well as its interrelatedness.

Market forces today: haphazard, dynamic and experimental.

'It hits you on the head and makes you think,' Nehru said of Corbusier's Chandigarh, 'and the one thing which India requires is being hit on the head so that it may think.'[2] The design of Chandigarh manifested an important strain in Nehru's complex idea of modern India: the sense that India had to cut loose from the contradictory modernity introduced by the British Raj – a modernity deformed by the weight of colonialism – just as it had also to free itself from a disabling nostalgia for a (selectively remembered) indigenous past. India had to move forward by one decisive act that broke with both its ancient and its colonial history. Chandigarh divested itself of history of any sort, rejecting both colonial pageantry and nationalist sentimentalism or ornament. It lacks the obligatory nationalist statuary and road-sign nomenclatura that pervades every other Indian city – Le Corbusier specifically banned all of this. The city's radical meaning lay in its cultural and physical unfamiliarity, its brazen assertion of the new and other. It conceded nothing to location or to surrounding culture. Instead it chose to celebrate a wholly alien form, style and material, and in doing so strove for a zero-degree condition that would make it equally unclaimable by any and every cultural or religious group. Just as the English language placed all Indians – at least in principle – at a disadvantage of equal unfamiliarity, so too Chandigarh did not lend itself to easy seizure or possession by any one group. Even those Indian elites who were familiar with colonial building idioms, with the bungalow and the verandah, were going to have to learn from scratch how to find their way around this brave new world of brise-soleils and reinforced concrete.

Such projections of the Indian idea emerged out of conversations between a no doubt restricted nationalist elite and currents of international Modernism: part of its purpose was to create a rhetorical pedagogy for society at large. It prompted a range of debates: for example, the protracted, sometimes self-indulgent but also fruitful argument about an 'Indian architecture', about the purpose, role, ambitions of building in and for India, the relation between past and present.

In surveying today's scene, one ready conclusion is to see a shift from an essentially state-defined vision, as set out in the decades of the 1950s and 1960s, to one defined by the market and capitalist forces today – inevitably more haphazard, but also more dynamic and experimental. Yet there are reasons to be sceptical about these latter qualities.

Today, it seems, there are two striking developments in the architectural realm that relate to the role of the state and of private capital. First, the national state has pulled back from projecting an idea of India through the built and physical environment. The major state-directed building projects, such as they are, are no longer destinations, but routes of approach: highways, flyovers, airports, telecommunications networks, electricity grids – the infrastructure. The way the state now represents itself is not through monumental edifices, but through its ability to steward statistics such as growth rates and social indicators: a new statistical architecture of state, through which it seeks to legitimate itself.

Approach routes are now the major state-directed building projects.

Second, private capital now chooses to build its own, self-generated and controlled habitats: their value lies precisely in the extent to which they are insulated from their surrounding environment. The information technology campus (ironically, itself created by the Nehruvian project) is the paradigm of this, existing as a parallel world. Yet unlike the steel cities of the 1950s and 1960s such as Bhilai, the denizens of such campuses are not involved in citizen-making. Rather, they take pride in the fact that they exist in international time zones, in an orbital relation to their immediate physical neighbours and surrounds. These are zones where the 'Non-Resident Indian' and the 'Resident Non-Indian' come together to converse in a bleached cosmopolitanism.

The retreat of the state as public builder, and the withdrawal of private capital into its protected, walled spaces, has meant the abdication of urban space as a site on which to debate and project conceptions of India.

Has any of this provoked any sort of debate or discussion about architecture in India? Not really. It is considered a brave and radical thing to suggest that the corporate world commission one of the usual architectural suspects to build in India: 'One can now afford to bring in a Renzo Piano, Frank Gehry, Richard Meier or even IM Pei,' writes a commentator in one of India's leading weeklies,[3] and no doubt soon enough someone will fly in one of the world's pomp-architects to construct a building, an offcut from a project destined for another global site. This is fine: but it is unlikely to make Indians think about their projects in the way Nehru had wished.

Astonishingly, there has been virtually no architectural debate around the two politically electric subjects, directly related to the built environment, that over the past 15 years or so have figured most vividly in the popular imagination. The first is the eruption of public statuary across the poor,

Hindi-speaking states of north India, of thousands of renderings of Dr BR Ambedkar, the leader of India's Dalits ('untouchables'). Erected at public expense, they seek to give public recognition and visibility to many millions of Indians who historically were kept invisible – even to themselves – by the caste system. The political currents pushing this represent a 'silent revolution' in India's democracy, and bring into the public realm meanings, dreams and energies that are already writing themselves into public space. The second is the rubble of the 16th-century Babri Masjid in Ayodhya, pickaxed in 1992 by Hindu activists supported by the Hindu nationalist party, the BJP, which now hopes to build a temple on this site. The Ayodhya wreckage represents the most serious challenge to the founding Indian project. The demand to build a temple there is couched in a language of continuity and tradition: in fact, it marks a rupture with India's past, an attempt at erasing centuries of history and cultural creation. It threatens a more profound break with the past than any seen in India's history. The future is creeping up on Indian architecture, even as the past still grasps it. Architecture as a mediation of, meditation upon, time – past, present and future – has in India lost this self-understanding and has excused itself from some of the most important arguments about what 'project India' might choose for itself. △

**Notes**
1. Tibor Mende, *Conversations with Mr. Nehru*, Secker & Warburg (London), 1956, p 63.
2. 'Speech at the seminar and exhibition on Architecture' New Delhi, in *Jawaharlal Nehru's Speeches, 1957–1963, vol 4*, Ministry of Information (New Delhi), 1964, p 176.
3. Gurcharan Das, 'Arise from the Clay Earth', *Outlook* magazine, 21 August 2006.

Text © 2007 John Wiley & Sons Ltd. Images: pp 12, 13(t), 14 © Kazi Ashraf; p 13(b) © Reinhold Martin; p 15 © Ramesh Biswas

# Indian
# Panorama

The architectural panorama, redolent of the multiplicity of India, shows fresh latitudes and accents. With software/IT as the talisman of contemporary India, it is not surprising that the new architectural debate will centre on the dualism of the yogi and the techie. Peter Eisenman, in an early foray into the debate, proposed the design for a software company in Bangalore in the early 1990s through a tensional coalition between tradition and technology, which he attempted by warping the mandala through wobbly Cartesian grids. The convenient duality of the yogi versus the techie sublimates but does not fully dissolve a vast and nuanced middle ground in the architectural production of India today. Earlier imperatives for a regional architecture, seen in some of the brilliant work of Balkrishna Doshi, Charles Correa, Raj Rewal, Ranjit Sabikhi and others, are now replaced by various competing inclinations and desires.

The context within which all this is happening is a turbulent one marked by social spasms, cultural ambiguities, economic reorientations and environmental adjustments. Global and transnational links challenge many of the precepts of post-independence, insular India. An unprecedented migratory experience (what the multimedia artist Shailja Patel calls 'migritude') impacts on a vast part of the subcontinent, creating new definitions of far and near, and ours and theirs. The resulting panorama exudes both indulgence and introspection, although it is clear that the motto 'excess is good' overshadows the traditional mode of reasonable and austere applications – something that might have pleased the Bollywood diva of the 1950s, Nargis, who had complained then of the representation of India through the films of Satyajit Ray that smacked only of abject poverty.

In this period of tumultuous transformations, when a new landscape is slowly but inexorably blanketing existing ones, and as sociologists, writers and poets are grappling with the nature of this phenomenon, architects are either having a field day mining the prospects of this new town, musing over the loss of the old ones (architectural writer Gautam Bhatia describes the current condition as a 'modernitis plague'), or retrenching to find a strategy to go forward. While large-scale building enterprises triggered by a globalised economy and desirous of an 'international standard' may be the most visible order of the day, architecture will continue to be spawned within geographic specificities and distinctive human conditions. The essayist Mulk Raj Anand's challenge to architects in 1962 regarding the possibilities unleashed by independence and industrialisation may haunt the new generation in whether they wish to be mere technicians or big *mistries* – hangers-on of the lower middle class – or refuse to accept the vision that was being thrust upon them by the new light. The projects featured in this section, whether by an architect in India, or an architect in a transnational tie with another in Europe, or an architect from New York or Singapore, offer new performances rather than being passive beneficiaries.

# Chris Lee/Kapil Gupta

With both its architects working from separate cities, Chris Lee/Kapil Gupta is the face of the increasing number of transnational practices now encompassing India, and evidence of the long-term international associations that architectural education now enables. Chris Lee Architects is an international practice based in London which is informed through research conducted at the Architectural Association, where Lee has taught since 2002. Gupta is design principal at Contemporary Urban India and the Director of Research and Publications at the Urban Design Research Institute, Mumbai. Being fascinated by the evolution and mutation of building types in today's cities, Lee and Gupta explore the issues that lie at the intersection between architecture and urbanism with a particular focus on developing new relevant types for these environments.

## Jewel Tech, Mumbai, 2002

In the design of this new diamond-cutting factory, the goal of the architects was to reverse the paranoia-inducing, prison-like conditions of a conventional factory. A 'reverse-panopticon' effect is thus proposed, whereby a glass canyon void works as a surveillance chamber, connecting the different departments and facilities. All circulation within the building is routed through this void. Surveillance is constant and visual rather than physical, removing the need for intrusive body searches, as was the case in older factories. Metal staircases that connect the different production levels are hung with cables so that they bounce with every step a craftsman takes though the void, resonating his movement and heightening his presence. Small openings throughout the whole factory take the form of light slits in the aluminium and glass-panel cladding.

## Fort School, Mumbai, 2005–

The challenge for the Fort School, located in the historical district of Kala Goda, was to redefine the organisation and functionality of a school vertically by adapting the core elements of a high-rise. Contrary to the sprawling low-rise block typology of a school surrounded by green fields, here the planning parameters for the district and the economic strategy of the school dictated a high-density, high-rise block. Five cores are distributed evenly across the floor plates to act as structural elements as well as circulation (the main core contains a continuous ramp). The perforated cores are generated as a series of elliptical undulations that thicken to form structural walls with openings for light and visibility. The facade is also conceived as a structural element, made up of a diamond grid to counter the stress along the large cantilevers.

## deGustibus, Mumbai, 2007

Here, a group of disused buildings from the colonial past set within the Mumbai Race Course are to be converted to form a series of food and beverage complexes. The conservation guidelines call for the preservation of the roof profile for three-quarters of the buildings, and full conservation for the remaining quarter. The stunning aspect of the site, however, is not the colonial buildings but the open spaces covered by mature rain trees. The proposed design attempts to further the idea of a continuous yet differentiated space with no clear boundary within the envelope of the conservation buildings. Creating a new structure within an old building envelope is achieved by adopting a kind of tree-branch system, whereby the Corten-clad roof is punctured with a series of openings that correspond to the intersection of the branches.

Text © 2007 John Wiley & Sons Ltd. Images © Kapil Gupta

# TEAM (Snehansu Mukherjee and AR Ramanathan)

With a practice based in New Delhi since 1985, TEAM has encountered the various swings in the architectural climate of India with a certain restraint and consistency by addressing issues of sustainability and conservation at all scales of design from architecture to settlement planning.

## Osho Dham, Najafgarh, bordering Gurgaon and Delhi, 1994–

The design for this commune for the followers of Osho (formerly Bhagwan Shree Rajneesh) takes into account its primary uses as a meditation camp and accommodation for the followers. The goal was to create a self-sustaining commune where vegetables and wheat are grown using organic fertilisers and pesticides. The various buildings, although grouped closely together, are separated through landscape design using groves of trees. The buildings' black exteriors mean they merge with the shadows of the surrounding trees.

## Ganguly Bakshi House, Faridabad, Haryana, 1994

One of the first houses to be constructed in a new development area on the border of Delhi, the building was designed, within a very tight budget, to resemble a little keep in a wilderness where herds of Nilgais roamed, and also so that it would eventually fit into a more developed suburban plot.

Text © 2007 John Wiley & Sons Ltd. Images © Team for Engineering Architecture and Management (TEAM)

# Sanjay Puri Architects

The diverse and prodigious work of Sanjay Puri Architects, based in Mumbai since 1992, embodies the new ebullient economy of India in the various townships, housing schemes, malls and new building types.

## Aishwarya at Baroda, Baroda, 1999

This group housing project provides affordable high-density accommodation, taking advantage of the openness and views, and large recreational areas, that such developments offer, yet generating the types of space that only individual low-rise houses normally possess. Sociological, physical and climatic factors of the region, and the behavioural patterns of the local people, informed the design. A large internal courtyard allows cross-ventilation and forms a cool area for playing and social gatherings during the harsh heat of summer. In addition, a spacious garden for outdoor activities also facilitates the processional celebration of the region's popular festival, Navratri, within the complex.

## Amby Valley Sahara Lake City Leisure Center (AVSLC), Lonavla, Maharashtra, 2003

Rather than creating partitioned spaces, the entire internal volume of this leisure centre is delineated into several platforms of varying heights. Since the location enjoys beautiful landscaped surroundings, it was important to ensure uninterrupted views from the interior spaces. Each area, such as the sports facilities, cafeteria, library, office, lounge and Internet café, is separated only by differentiated ground levels, allowing the natural outdoors to be visible from the interior. Each level is bound by low wood partitions that move fluidly within the internal volume, creating an abstract formation. Floating trapezoidal panels in the ceiling, suspended at varying levels, enhance the meandering formation of the low partitions.

Text © 2007 John Wiley & Sons Ltd. Images: p 20(t) © Sanjay Puri Architects, photo Vinesh Gandhi; p 20(b) © Sanjay Puri Architects

# Fabian Ostner

Fabian Ostner represents a new transnational practice triggered by the experimental and international environment at Auroville which attracts architects from all over the world. Trained in Germany, and having worked in Berlin and Mumbai, Ostner now runs his practice from the former French colony of Pondicherry, a city in south India close to both Auroville and Chennai. He cites the reason for his architectural domicile in India as the charter of Auroville, in its striving to represent a bridge between past and present and, ultimately, human unity. Ostner focuses on bridging traditional building culture with a modern approach to architecture that is often conveyed by his compelling projective images.

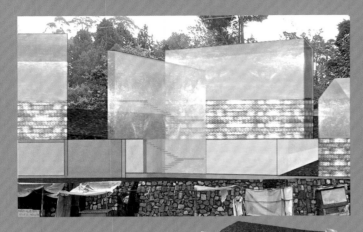

## Kodaikanal Hotel and Spa, Kodaikanal, Tamil Nadu, 2004

The proposed site for a hotel-cum-spa in the hill station of Kodaikanal in south India, famous for its climate, forests, plantations and the lake in the town centre, is adjacent to the lake and has beautiful old trees growing on its slopes. Any new construction in Kodaikanal must respect strict building bylaws, and in this case new buildings would be permissible only in place of existing ones, must not exceed two storeys, and would have to feature sloped roofs. Keeping in mind these regulations, a large part of the programme (pool, spa, gym, parking, utilities) is placed below ground, partially using the slope to look out on to the green landscape and the lake. Above ground, the new buildings emerge from the outlines of the previous ones and house the hotel rooms and dining facilities.

As delivery of materials to the town is problematic, the design foresees the prefabrication of most elements and a fast assembly on site. The buildings are made of steel frames and clad in glass to achieve a maximum exchange between inside and out.

## Midford Garden, Bangalore, 2003

The design team for this corporate head office for a textile manufacturer in Bangalore also included Brand New Day and Dominic Dube. The design wraps around part of the existing buildings on the site, and the architecture is clear and simple, in contrast to the somewhat chaotic development in the area. Ground-floor spaces are open to the public and house boutiques and an auditorium.

Text © 2007 John Wiley & Sons Ltd. Images © Fabian Ostner

# Tod Williams Billie Tsien Architects

The work of the New York-based practice of Tod Williams Billie Tsien Architects is well known for producing lyrical designs that are materially rich and spatially innovative. The terms 'humanity' and 'poetic quality' have been regularly used in reviewing their numerous residential and institutional projects. The context of an Indian project provides a new opportunity for the finely crafted, tactile architecture the practice is known for.

### Banyan Park, Mumbai, 2003–

Among the new buildings and campuses emerging from the economic upswing in India, the Banyan Park campus for Tata Consultancy Services (TCS) explores the grouping and relationship of buildings in the tropical milieu of Mumbai alongside innovations in fabrication. The 9-hectare (23-acre) campus is located on a site near Mumbai's international airport. The project, designed with associate architects Somaya & Kalappa Consultants, comprises 12 separate buildings that are interconnected by shaded passageways that provide shelter from Mumbai's intense heat and seasonal monsoons. Concrete and local stone will be used extensively to give a sense of permanence and mass, and generous windows will let in light and views where needed, avoiding large expanses of glass curtain-wall.

The project is intended to be experienced on foot, and passage between the different buildings of the campus is under cover in the open air. Numerous paths allow pedestrians to either jog or stroll, and the landscape has been designed to create both open areas of grass and trees and quiet contemplative courtyards.

Within the buildings, the hallways are also outdoor spaces, this time connected by generous exterior stairs that encourage people to move from floor to floor on foot; places to sit and talk overlooking the verdant landscape will be incorporated into the walkways – a planning approach that also greatly reduces cooling demands and energy use.

The buildings are also connected by raised passageways, one of which, located at the entrance to the campus, is a pedestrian bridge that will be clad with large stone *jalis* (perforated screens). These reinterpretations of traditional Indian hand-carved panels provide another way to filter light and frame views of the campus.

The offices are configured around a series of central courtyards. Elliptical openings in the roof will provide diffuse light to the centre of each courtyard, bringing a gentle light into the work spaces. Additional light will come from windows with large horizontal stone sunshields. Keenly aware of the problems of glare, the work spaces have thus been designed to allow views to the outside while shielding the inside from direct light.

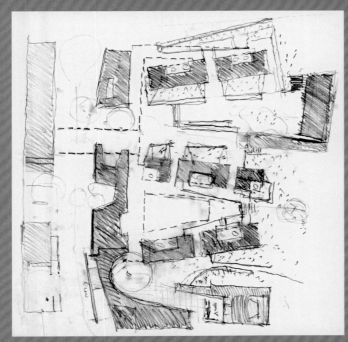

Text © 2007 John Wiley & Sons Ltd. Images © Tod Williams Billie Tsien Architects, LLP

# One Space, Many Worlds

'Cities hold two-thirds of their residents in slums, and the rest in stiflingly limiting, inflexible structures.' Thus the impoverished parochial Mumbai is one and the same metropolis as the cosmopolitan globalised 'Bombay'. **Ramesh Biswas** examines how the speculative housing developments of the aspirational middle classes are creating townships that intensify sprawl and further decentralise cities, squandering the potential for upgrading public space and creating an architecture for the common good.

Plotted development on a citywide scale: outdated planning laws have nonetheless failed to create coherent, connected urban quarters.

SLOAP (Space Left Over After Planning) between office buildings becomes vibrant people space, creating an informal economic network.

At cocktail parties a favourite topic of conversation is the punishment-posting that the typically nomadic guests – diplomats, managers, consultants and tourists – have undergone. Invariably, the most absurd, shudder-inducing stories are of Indian cities: the decaying infrastructure, the crumbling superstructure, the visible air, the daily near-catastrophes, the brown polyester safari suits! Jan Morris memorably referred to Delhi as the world capital of the missed appointment, the wrong number and the punctured tyre. How does this synchronise with the jubilation about 'emerging India', an India of high growth, hi-tech and high returns?

A fairground of monsters and miracles, India-town is different from other boomtowns. Don't be fooled by the plethora of cranes and confuse it with China. In an urban geography both buildings and the ideology and imagery encasing them create their own specific reality, deviating from the global patterns they apparently follow, requiring a closer look at location. Nissel and Mehrotra have postulated the existence of a Bombay (a Westward-looking, globalised, fragmented entity) and a Mumbai (a more parochial, resistant network) in the same space, each with its own economy, politics and pantheon of images. Cities old and new – Delhi, Chandigarh or Jaipur – are manifestations of power frozen in stone, where static, monumental mass fixed in space defines the city. In others, famously Bombay, it is not space that is at work as the paramount infrastructure, but time that is the major order-giver and organiser of events – of transience, fluidity, ecstasy, phantasmagoria and disillusionment.

'Three Different Poses in Three Different Modern Dresses' boasts a photo studio signboard. Images and representations have as much to do with the production of architecture as do underlying material conditions. In today's consumer world, new aesthetic ideologies will inevitably be layered into conventional models. Architectural heterogeneity would merely reflect prevailing cultural heterogeneity. But there are

different kinds of 'chaos' – new Indian architecture lacks the sheer fun of Kuala Lumpur, Shanghai or Tokyo, and settles instead for clichés and monuments to boredom. It is less a case of fusion, and more one of missing the point. Branding has replaced thinking, status has replaced taste, and American real-estate jargon has been adopted wholeheartedly. What remains is second-hand Vegas/Dubai, themselves marketplaces of Xeroxed 3-D images.

'Change your clothes, change your lifestyle,' drive after a work day in your 'Seattle-style' office to your 'English Country Club', your 'Egyptian Mall', your 'Mykonos Sports Centre', your 'Swiss Chalet' or 'Hacienda House' in an 'Australian Gated City' or even a 'Prairie Paradise Park' (quotes from this week's advertisements – down payments accepted upfront). A zoo of copycat styles, these new Bollywood Baroque 'townships' are a source of hilarity. Maybe the need for denial and escape from the harsh realities of climate, crowds and crime is real, and architecture has to assist Bollywood in meeting it. These hybrid 'elsewheres' with glittery fronts and stone-age plumbing are testimonials to the absolute failure of a developer-driven market to provide a contemporary, innovative or even appropriate urban environment, and to the

Holy cow! Glocalisation.

Malls threaten Mom-and-Pop stores, but informal services flourish illegally in the interstices between legally questionable projects.

lack of technical standards, talent and ethics of the thousands of architects who provide the designs.

How does one explain the paradox that urbanism as a profession has practically disappeared at the very moment it is needed the most, with cities quadrupling their populations within a generation? While architects tend to concentrate on the individual building and then jump straight to the global, leaving out a whole range of levels – urban spatial and social contexts, and regional characteristics – sociologists tend to ignore the physical world and tell us little about cities as places. Again, economists relate to statistics and miss the role of outstanding individuals or the seduction of glamorous form. However, while space must be filled out with architecture if meaningful models of cities are to emerge, buildings cannot be theorised out of their economic or cultural context. It is thus useful to look at significant specifics of Indian urban history to understand today's city.

No statistic is flogged more frequently than the one purporting 80 per cent of India to be rural, thus repressing the reality of a thoroughly urban economy. India, like China, Turkey, Iran or the Arab world is a fundamentally urban civilisation with peripheral rural settlements. Archaeological and genealogical evidence shows that it was the collapse of the Indus Valley civilisation, with its urban characteristics (zones of production and trade, division of labour, non-subsistence activity, and places of learning) that led to the subsequent formation of villages. Later, Ahmedabad was India's largest precolonial city, one of several with a flourishing mix of magnificent ensembles and deeply urban cultures.

Today, 'small' towns of millions are everywhere, but even apparently rural settlements are typologically urban. Any village is bound to the urban economy with supply chains, every 'rural' family has members working in cities to support them, and consumer patterns or the ubiquitous television screen bring urban values to the remotest hut – in short, only tribal peoples are genuinely 'non-urban'. The acceptance of

Isolated malls with poor transport connectivity are used as air-conditioned family picnic destinations. Purchases are still largely made in cheaper neighbourhood markets.

New Bombay: unconnected developer projects, lacking a centre, or even a central idea.

Switzerland is not what it used to be: a housing estate advertised as 'Swiss Cottages'.

this fact would enable more focused policy, as the city stretches into the countryside.

Notably, the transformation of inner cities so evident worldwide has not come to India: the suggestion to replace crumbling, substandard structures with socially and ecologically responsive buildings, or to upgrade urban spaces, is met with incomprehension. As India continues to open up economically, the hinterland is duplicating the functions of the untouched centre. Urban growth happens in speculative, concept-free complexes (or should one say 'simplexes'), in ever-increasing circles around cities. These private housing estates, SEZs (special economic zones) and office parks represent the withdrawal of money from public space and shared institutions, its use for private services and the creation of new caste-territories that bypass the common good. Infrastructure is left to the overburdened state. Building

regulations? Officials look the other way, or even invest their ill-gained 'pocket money' in these projects. The choice of planners is not a result of architectural competition, but a by-product of nepotism, corruption or subcontracting relationships. The multicentred city is emerging, not as a deliberate strategy to decentralise, but as accidental sprawl, seamlessly welding cities as far apart as Delhi, Chandigarh, Gurgaon, Jaipur and Agra. We need to say farewell to the traditional image of the city with a tight, accessible centre, a recognisable skyline of domes and towers, central business functions or sidewalk cafés, and learn to accept the emerging reality of a continuous, undifferentiated two- to four-storeyed sprawl of cubes and anonymous sheds extending for hundreds of kilometres, punctuated by suburban bunches of high-rise offices and gated apartments. People will live, study and work somewhere in this pulsating mass without ever coming to Connaught Place – though there may well be Sunday bus excursions to Lutyen's Capitol, now the museal centre of a 'Greater Gurgaon'.

What suffers is the quality of design, the match to users and climate, and the evolution of a vibrant, original contemporary architecture beyond Disney-like pastiches. But if this exopolitan restructuring is inevitable, efforts must be made to develop a new landscape urbanism for it.

To list the meagre handful of buildings that attempt a new vernacular would only draw attention to the pathetic general state of affairs. A leading Indian architect, confronted with the dearth of world-class contemporary architecture in India while even much smaller countries have more to show, blamed construction companies and corruption. True, the system is detrimental to good building – no certification of contractors means that just about anybody can declare himself one, hire people from his village, effectively enslave them with loans, and put them on site without rudimentary training or supervision. Add to that low pay and miserable treatment – does anyone really expect a shantytown dweller to produce fine buildings? The depressing new townships and institutional campuses (have they just been constructed or are they just being demolished?) are as puzzling as the dull synthetic safari suits worn in a country bursting with explosively coloured, natural materials.

Though Indian architects lament that only a fraction of construction involves their services, the 'unplanned' bazaar is really more vibrant and full of exhilarating surprises than the organised sector. Indeed, the British decision to bypass scarily inscrutable and seemingly chaotic cores to build cantonments and capitols on green fields is one reason why colonial rule did not destroy the indigenous urban heritage of India as it did elsewhere. The British failed to see that the apparent chaos in the streets of Old Delhi, Bhopal or Rawalpindi was nothing of the sort, but actually a complex rhizome-like layering of strictly defined functions and structures. Exactly who could use which square foot of space at what time of the day was, and is, strictly regulated and nothing was left to chance – really, nothing could be more organised.

But however old a country's urban history, it would be a mistake to rely solely on tradition, as architecture is rarely autochthonous. International influences and adaptive exchange are crucial to architectural growth. Never mind the 'foreign' nature of Mogul architecture that fused Iranian spatial proportions with Indian craft traditions to produce some of the finest buildings the world knows. Arguably, most of India's remarkable works of the 20th century were also the result of foreign intervention: grand colonial buildings, Kahn's Management Institute, Le Corbusier's Mill Owner's Association Building, Art Deco villas by architects who fled Europe, charity projects, parts of Auroville or Chandigarh, and the Lotus Temple.

For decades, the closed economy hindered professionals and decision-makers from travelling and measuring themselves against developments elsewhere and prevented crucial technological or know-how transfer. Today's unusually high returns have resulted in a gold rush to India, whose place in the geopolitical economy is nowhere as strong as China's; however, investors see greater profits and legal security in India, despite slow decision-making and permits. Yet the fundamental flaws in this boom are manifold. India does not appear to be absorbing badly needed infusions of know-how, quality and technology that come with foreign investment, something that the 'tiger states' of Southeast Asia made use of a decade ago to modernise their cities. Guaranteed sales leave developers without any motivation to improve quality. Land is valued more than the compensatorily cheap building on it. Little thought is given to climate responsiveness to increase comfort within house and cluster, and cut costs and emissions. Energy efficiency via intelligent sections is still unknown. The absence of insulation or double-glazing increases air-conditioning load, although it is known that globally the energy used to cool buildings far exceeds that needed to heat them. Primitive installations waste scarce water and electricity, and money for constant repairs. Instead of adopting technically sound best practices, it is superficial style that is copied, resulting in *khichri* (an amorphously stodgy porridge). The slavish use of wasteful glass-aluminium facade systems is ubiquitous, though these would no longer meet the stringent standards of their Western countries of origin. Contemporary adaptation of local or new materials, or of urban configurations, is rarely seen outside research institutes and student projects. And where are the modern masterpieces that exploit the unique quality of light?

Residential design is time-frozen, still offering tired 19th-century 'drawing room, dining room, master bedroom' configurations rather than flexible spaces to enable various ways of living and working for the multigenerational family

Demand and marketing ensure sky-high prices for third-rate housing.

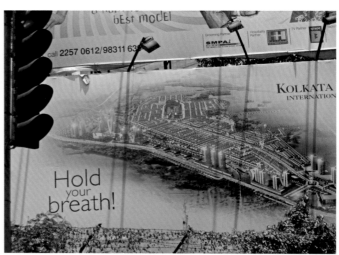
Don't hold your breath!

Lego and Xerox as urban design tools. The aim appears to be an escape as far away from India as imaginable.

or the single night-time call-centre employee. Increasing numbers of diasporic 'Non-Resident Indians' and non-Indians in the workforce create new living and leisure patterns, as do microglobalisation and the uncoupling of 'location' and 'milieu'.

There is little study of how Indians negotiate urban spaces, how they perceive the city. Yet an understanding of the rapidly changing ways people eat, consume, meet, play or trade off space, accessibility, amenity and self-image is crucial to the design of essentially (as opposed to superficially) 'regional Indian' urban environments. Instead of uniformly gloomy 'real-estate projects', outdated before they are complete, we could arrive at livable cities.

Builder-developers, architects, governments, brokers or environmentalists all follow their own smug trajectories, desperate chess players pitched against a fast-moving computer, and it will take time before consensual commonalities are worked out – after all, it has taken Europe decades after the Second World War, or indeed since the French Revolution and the Enlightenment to reach its intra-urban balance of interests. However, those concepts of equal rights and reason, of a genuine balance of individual excellence and common goals, are yet to inform Indian urbanity, just as the rights of the individual are stifled by 'tradition', obscurantism and patriarchal structures, despite lip service to modernisation.

The city has always meant liberation from social shackles and discrimination – a place to make money, yes, but above all a place to realise one's own potential. If one didn't want to marry the man one's grandmother chose, or work in one's uncle's shop, the only escape was the city, with all its possibilities and dreams. The very process of urbanisation has done more for women than affirmative action policy. Ethnic subgroups and international workers are commendably integrated today, largely without conflict. Yet the absence of the emancipatory project is painfully evident. Cities hold two-thirds of their residents in slums, and the rest in stiflingly limiting, inflexible structures. How can young adults realise their potential if forced to live with their parents and accept family dictates, merely for lack of an alternative on the residential market? The sooner those responsible shed knee-jerk protectionism to realise these flaws, the faster the infusion of quality. All these deficits are starting points, potential fields for improvement towards a culturally sustainable, modern urban India.

German television used to fill the night-time screen with silent transmissions from a spacecraft and, possibly equally alien, an aerial view of a Delhi traffic junction where camel carts carrying satellite dishes competed with 30 forms of transport moving in 18 different directions. Yet no one got hurt, and it may be symbolic of the negotiating talent that keeps the Indian city going, albeit at a slow pace and high inefficiency. Indeed it is astounding (and shaming) how, despite the collective failure of professionals and municipalities, Indian cities defiantly disprove all prognoses of their decline or of their sheer impossibility. Flying on autopilot, they and their citizens overcome shortcomings by coping and innovating with incredible, often illegal, energy. Like Baron Münchhausen they grab their own pigtails to pull themselves out of the mire. While all cities are fascinatingly complex, Indian cities are uniquely so in their variegated cacophony, wild juxtapositions of eras and cultures, and unexpected glimpses of great beauty and warmth. In the midst of frustrations and wasted potential, there are moments of joy, humour and humanity – these are not disaster zones, but crucibles of hope and progress. ◮

Text © 2007 John Wiley & Sons Ltd. Images © Ramesh Biswas

# The Visceral City and the Theatre of Fear

Over the last decade in India, intensive urbanisation, with the aid of the mass media, has unleashed a new culture of fear. Widespread access to TV, text messaging and the Internet have heightened and played upon individuals' anxieties. **Ravi Sundaram** describes how in Delhi, in particular, the media provided the catalyst for 'mass hysteria' and 'psychosis' during the summer of 2002.

**Monica Narula, *Night Vision*, Sarai Media Lab, Delhi, 2004**
This photocomposition sets up the imaginary tempo of the global city at night with light (neon, consumption) overwhelming the dark city.

**Monica Narula, *Traffic*, Sarai Media Lab, 2004**
Night traffic in the postcolonial city suggests claustrophobia and the danger of contingent death, overwhelming the global city of light.

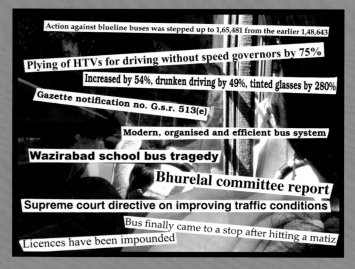

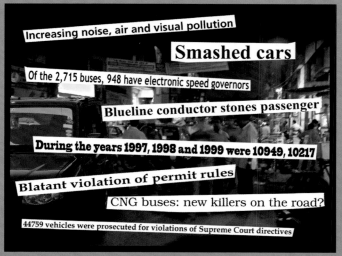

**Mrityunjay Chatterjee, *The Sensorium 1*, Sarai Media Lab, 2006**
In the first work in a series that uses a montage of newspaper headlines and photographic form, Chatterjee images the sensorial effects of the media on Delhi during the 1990s. Here he sets up a force field with accident headlines and government and judicial reports.

**Mrityunjay Chatterjee, *The Sensorium 2*, Sarai Media Lab, 2006**
In this montage, the artist mixes statistics, dangerous machines and death – a common experience of the visceral city in the 1990s.

Walter Benjamin's suggestion in the 1920s that 'the collective is also corporeal' intimated the mix of image, technology and experience that has defined contemporary cities. Benjamin's idea of a corporeal urban experience suggests an increasing entanglement of body and technology, where city dwellers process a range of shock-like visual stimuli, and develop disciplining techniques to deal with distraction, as well as tactile, playful appropriations of the rush of images. This changed phenomenology of nearness and distance brought about by the media has an equally dark, visceral quality, tearing apart stable modes of contemplation. The dramatic 'live' experience brought about by flickering film, television, advertising and mobile screens also disperses space, bringing new dangers, anxieties and phobias. In the context of postcolonial South Asia, where the media and urban boom have evolved together in recent years, fear has become implicated in a broader social theatre of urbanity.

The emergence of a media-urbanism in contemporary Indian cities has thrown into confusion technologies of government management of populations. As postcolonial cities expand turbulently in many parts of the world, media experiences increasingly expose and generate new sites of fear. In Indian cities, such sites include paranoia about strangers, middle-class pathologies of crime, and significant public expressions of 'irrational' and non-modern fears. As events are instantly relayed – through popular rumour, text messages, mobile phone photos and media headlines – fear proliferates in everyday life, moving beyond its classic location in the experience of the uncanny.

We may consider this phenomenon from two vantage points: the technologies of fear and danger, and the experience of the 'event'. Technologies of fear refers to the knowledge and techniques deployed to manage, map and understand urban fear in contemporary cities. These technologies emerge from specific sites of power: urban government, police, hospitals, courts, civic groups, professional bodies and media managers. The new technologies of fear are innovative, intervening through media effects: publicised court judgements, TV campaigns, new physiognomies of identification and information gathering. Rather than care for a social body, today the language of risk and uncertainty is the favoured terrain for technologies of fear. The 'event' works through its own landscape of effects: popular rumour, media coverage and the marking of space by the urban poor. The 'event' inhabits diverse social and media spaces, moving between the body of the crowd, traffic, neighbourhoods, and also in the material traffic of images and objects. It is the ability to move rapidly between unequal social groups, spaces and media that gives the contemporary experience of urban fear an edgy, neurological feeling.

### Time of the 'Global'
Globalisation significantly blurred the lines between the media and the urban experience for millions of city dwellers in India. In contrast to the earlier decades, the 1990s generated a series of fast-moving material and tactile media. Low-cost computers, advertising, mobile phones, and digital images have transformed urban life. The media-urbanism of contemporary India seems to have now gone well beyond Benjamin's pioneering media anthropology of the urban senses. At one level, the experience after the early 1990s is now a more global one, incorporating design, telecom networks, architecture, media industries, service workers, personal media objects and multiple sensory environments. The development of new suburbia notwithstanding, media-urbanism in Delhi has lacked the spectacular force of its Western and East Asian counterparts, operating instead as a continuous immersion into a world of low-cost (new) and pirate media forms drawing millions of urban dwellers into the dream world of images.

What is significant is the emergence of new forms of publicity: images now crowd streets, walls and buses; electronically boosted soundscapes (music, political campaigns, religious chants, car horns) expand and occupy roads and neighbourhood space. Interestingly this kinetic media sensorium is often experienced in mixed spaces – low-cost video players in working-class areas running makeshift movie theatres. In short, Delhi in the 1990s combined urban expansion and crisis along with an overwhelming world of new media experiences.

### Scene One: Managing Fear – Crisis, Risk and Technique
Anthony Vidler has argued that modern urbanism has always been haunted by Enlightenment fears of 'dark space',[1] which is seen as a repository of superstition, non-reason and the breakdown of civility. 'Dark space' constantly invades 'light space' through the fear of epidemics, urban panic, the homeless multitude and criminal activity.

This fear was partly echoed in postcolonial urbanism in Delhi. The new master plan for Delhi in the 1950s led to the formulation of an ambitious planning strategy. While the master plan continued colonial fears of congestion, its departure lay in the reorganisation of the relationship between space and subjectivity. While acknowledging nationalist sovereignty and the pressure to build a modern city, it was marked by an anxiety about the sources of urban citizenship in a non-Western society. The city was designed as a healthy body of 'proper' urban trade and industry, and those associated with the rural were to be slowly eased out.

The formal-legal framework of the master plan and its timid forecasts of Delhi's growth began to come apart in the late 1970s. By the 1990s, following major migrations as in Mumbai, a feeling of crisis and constant breakdown in the city exposed the inadequacies of the master plan. Suggesting the failure of its imaginary of ordered development, the bulk of Delhi's residents now live in non-legal neighbourhoods: ranging from working-class settlements to elite usurpations of public space. After the early 1990s, locations of the crisis moved on to different landscapes: the liberal environmentalist demand to remove 'polluting industries' from the city, public transportation and the alarmingly high rates of death on the road, and the general paranoia over terrorism and security after the wars in Kashmir and the Punjab. The main pressure was felt by the political arrangements of the urban regime. This had accommodated the great expansion of the non-legal city in the 1980s, often with the help of local politicians. Since the 1990s, this older 'political' model of urban growth has been thrown into complete confusion. A significant cause of this has been a middle-class environmental civic campaign that petitioned sympathetic courts, portraying the city as a space on the brink of ecological collapse and transport disaster.

The public enactment of crisis in Delhi in the 1990s led to a decisive shift in the language of urban governance. The predictions of danger and risk assessment now emerged from a new domain of experts not accountable to the elected city government. This marked a big shift from the planner era when experts reported to the city and national government. The Supreme Court appointed the new experts during pollution case hearings on petitions filed by civic activists. The court case became a giant 'event scene' in the city, with wide-ranging media effects involving experts, judges and affected populations, with the new experts promoting techniques that embrace and accelerate the media experience.

Differing from the more prominent techniques of surveillance and control that have emerged in response to war, terrorism and social conflict, urban risk techniques in postcolonial Delhi intimate a future that is fraught with both media intervention and conflict. While the earlier language of urbanism had suggested that the body be mapped, enumerated and disciplined to maintain its health, the new technologies of risk suggest that the problems of the city need to be resolved by bypassing the language of the social. Risk techniques suggest that urbanism's great wager in using Modern architecture and planning to produce disciplined healthy subjects can no longer control the problem of fear. While the older 1950s planner simply bypassed the catastrophe of the Partition in Delhi, the risk experts – the new barons of power – plunge actively into the theatre of danger and fear.

### Scene Two: Fear and the Event
More than most other Indian cities, Delhi has an unredeemed debt to its dead. In the 20th century, the Partition of 1947 led to large-scale killings of Muslims in the city, and in 1984 Congress workers organised a massacre of Sikhs following the assassination of Indira Gandhi. There are no memorials for the dead of these previous generations, nor any official commemorations. The memories survive in fugitive ways: stray literary reflections, personal stories handed down by old residents, a ghostly archive that leaves its traces in the various ruins that dot the city. For the most part the new planned city that emerged after the 1950s turned its back on the dead, the affective world of memory finding little place in the language of the master plan. It was the urban crisis of the 1990s that released the ghosts of the dead from the confinement of planning.

In the second volume of *The Practice of Everyday Life*, Michel de Certeau wrote: 'The debris of shipwrecked histories still today raise up the ruins of an unknown, strange city. They burst forth within the modernist, massive homogenous city like slips of the tongue from an unknown, perhaps unknown language.'[2] The city of death returned to haunt the new residents of the city in different guises, using de Certeau's notion of the 'unknown' language. Between the hot months of April and June 2001, the capital was deluged by stories of a monkey-like creature that attacked people at night. These stories emerged almost entirely from the proletarian and lower-middle-class neighbourhoods of eastern Delhi and the nearby suburbs of Ghaziabad and NOIDA. The first reports from local papers spoke of a *kala bandar* (black monkey). By May this black monkey had morphed into the figure of the 'monkeyman', a human–animal hybrid who displayed considerable speed, spreading violence and fear.

The monkeyman event almost immediately generated a frenzy of media effects with regular television and news reports, daily sightings and interviews with victims of perceived attacks. The Delhi police, harassed by hoax calls,

Mrityunjay Chatterjee, *The Sensorium 3*, Sarai Media Lab, 2006
The third work in the series mixes sensational headlines with dark humour, capturing the mix of technology, modern magic and fear that accompanied the monkeyman events.

Raqs Media Collective, Delhi, 28.28 N / 77.15 E :: 2001/02 (Co-Ordinates of Everyday Life, Delhi, 2002)
Stills from the installation first shown at Documenta 11, Kassel, Germany, from June to September 2002, using four projections, soundscape, slide projection and print elements (including broadsheet, floor mat and 18 types of sticker).

quickly set up a monetary reward for any information on the alleged nocturnal intruder, and also undertook massive patrolling of the streets in eastern Delhi on a scale seen only in response to major social disturbances. The police commissioner set up an enquiry committee of psychologists and forensic experts to probe the events. For almost two months the city was paralysed by news of the sightings, of four people dead, and of emergency rooms in government hospitals in eastern Delhi treating people who claimed to have encountered the nocturnal figure for shock and injury. By mid-June the stories seemed to have subsided, the police 'crack team' submitting in its report that the attacks stemmed from 'mass hysteria' and a 'fear psychosis'.

The events of the summer of 2001 present a puzzling dualism. If at one level media commentaries, senior police officials, rationalist campaigners and psychologists asserted that the affected populace was under the grip of rumour and mass delusion, the narratives from the subaltern parts of the city suggested the exact opposite. Ordinary citizens, residents of working-class settlements, urban villages and lower-middle-class colonies continued to assert the existence of the monkeyman as a verifiable source of fear. This perception found its way into local police narratives and medicolegal reports recorded in the emergency rooms of hospitals.

The new technologies of fear based on risk prediction and media saturation are but one response to the urban crisis. The incidents of the summer of 2001 posed a serious problem for this model of management: so excessive was the representational and affective world of the event(s) that it was not easily amenable to modern forms of criminal profiling or

new techniques of expert intervention and control. It can be argued that the events took the form of postcolonial haunting. Fugitive practices of seeing and believing, misogyny of animal and human, and the emergence of evil and danger in open spaces produced a flood that burst through the discourse of medical science and rationalism, suspending the ordinary operations of law and order. The subaltern neighbourhoods of eastern Delhi mobilised a terrifying imaginary of urban fear that intimated in a sudden flash a vision of the city as both a productive and hellish present.

The postcolonial city's wager on rational planning as well as its role as a model of assimilated urban citizenship has come apart in recent years. The great terror of disorder and the psychic unknown of the non-rational has been unleashed with globalisation rather than from non-modern pasts. While the language of risk expertise took this paranoid zone as a productive space for discursive intervention and enactment, events like the monkeyman panic temporarily inscribed a new subaltern geography of fear. While risk sought to manage the urban sensorium, the 'event' produced disturbing counter-memories and untimely acts that could not find a place in the catalogue of official media representation. ∆

**Notes**
1. Anthony Vidler, *The Architectural Uncanny: Essays in the Modern Unhomely*, MIT Press (Cambridge, MA), 1992.
2. Michel de Certeau, *The Practice of Everyday Life, Vol 2*, University of Minnesota Press (Minneapolis), 1998, p 133.

Text © 2007 John Wiley & Sons Ltd. Images: p 30(t) © Monica Narula; pp 30(b), 32 © Mrityunjay Chatterjee; p 33 © Raqs Media Collective

# Mumbai Architects

Mumbai (Bombay) is the undisputed 'world city' in every sense. While it is a miniature cosmos of India, Mumbai is also perched precariously on the shores of the subcontinent, unlike the deeply ensconced Delhi or Kolkata, reflecting an extroversion and daring that are particularly its own. Since the late 19th century, its great Indian middle class, representing a social dynamic of Mumbai, has encouraged and embraced the fruits of consumption and globalisation, typically ignoring traditional state or cultural austerities. If this cosmos be true in its multitudinous humanity, in the glitter of a world city, in its dream-manufacturing centres such as Bollywood and various couture houses, so is the fact that half its population lives in slums and on sidewalks (grippingly rendered in Suketu Mehta's urban paean *The Maximum City* and Greg Roberts' para-autobiography *Santaram*). The equation is made further lopsided by the cores of power that are constituted by an invisible and visible conglomerate of developers, financiers and politicians who control one of the most expensive real estates in the world without a particular urban plan or vision.

What is it like to be an architect in a turbulent site for the production of desires? It is one thing to be merely practising from this city, another thing to be learning from it, and quite another to be channelling its course. Rahul Mehrotra, whose projects are featured in this section, says that Mumbai, where his practice is based, provides him with a mine for quarrying architectural ideations and languages. In the incomparable multiplicity of the city, including its interminable extremities, architecture must find a plan for dialogue and inclusion. Younger architects such as Kapil Gupta (see the 'Indian Panorama' section) unravel opportunities where a received urban type is mutated, or types are combined into new radical combinations (for example, his Fort School project), accelerating the process of how the city constantly revises itself. Other architects making a mark in the city are Nuru Karim, Quaid Dongerwalla and Rahul Gore. Mumbai also belongs to Sanjay Puri Architects (see 'Indian Panorama') whose prodigious productions reflect the excessive desires of this world city. It is a fact, too, that its architecture has been oddly popularised by the enormously productive Hafeez Contractor, whose work ranges from daring speculations to speculative mimicries.

The projects in this section embody a tectonic clarity, landscape consciousness, elegance of construction and craft, and material sensuality without seeking sanctions in symbols and signs. They neither invoke the tottering certainty of archaism nor the inevitability of the excess, but instead the assuredness of a fine built work. Bijoy Jain, of Studio Mumbai Architects, in an office situated in a recycled rice warehouse in a rather vivacious and frayed part of town, curiously produces elegant and poetic forms for idyllic settings. With a discernible nod to the language of a tropical Asian modernity, the work of Rahul Mehrotra seeks a distillation of architecture to its elemental forms. Samira Rathod, practising a similar art and sharing some of the same language, is, however, not reticent about the nexus of developers and politicians in this city of marketable desires and ponders: Where is the criticism? And where is the resistance? The insurgency?

# Studio Mumbai Architects (Bijoy and Priya Jain)

Studio Mumbai Architects presents an exquisite architectural *poiesis* through the crafting or weaving of the building with the landscape, and the crafted fabrication of the building itself. The result is a choreographed architecture, compelling also in its Zen-like sparseness and delightful elegance. The intense sensuality of the practice's work is palpable without ideological mediation, through the modulation of light, material crafts, tactility, contrasting colours, and a heightened awareness of the site. Seeking 'tradition' through materiality and crafting, the architects incorporate 'local' construction techniques as a Modernist aestheticisation of the unselfconscious tradition.

Secret gardens, structures embedded in the landscape inviting flexible uses, materials that interact with garden, sky and weather, and the transformative effects of time (weathering) are just some of the terms of engagement for the work of Studio Mumbai. Very few architects since Geoffrey Bawa have established such a compelling and instructive relationship with the landscape, as this requires the patient botanical metaphor of cultivation. The question of landscape is not just a pictorial one, but one that must be substantiated by ecological and sustainable programmes.

Directed by Bijoy and Priya Jain, Studio Mumbai is a collaborative, multidisciplinary firm integrating architecture, landscape and interior design with product and furniture design. With a focus on crafting, the practice maintains its own established, year-round fabrication facilities in two locations where the timber structures, finished carpentry and furniture are handcrafted for each of its projects. Here, teams of skilled craftspeople, many originating from a long lineage of regional artisans, collaborate in a flexible and highly precise manufacturing process.

## Hiremath House, Kashid, Murud, 2006

This house explores concentric layers of privacy, its centre an open
courtyard garden that is meant to be traversed and occupied
intermittently throughout the day. The hierarchy of the layout is
concentric and circular rather than linear, encouraging a sequence
of gradual discovery. The structure forms an enclosure to house an
enchanted garden, which is the heart of the project. Ocean breezes
enter through a porous wood screen, and a courtyard pool is
screened by greenery, passageways and secret stairs leading up to
the roof or down to an underground well beneath the courtyard.

## Shroff House, Bandra, Mumbai, 2004–

A screen made of varying densities of timber slats wraps all sides of this glass house in an urban condition. The screen lets in views of the sky and trees while obscuring views from the street, and also functions as a lattice for hanging vines and bougainvillea cascading down from the roof top. Sliding glass doors and operable windows surround the house, connecting interior spaces to the outside elements. The bedrooms on the top floor of the four-level house form a courtyard with a central water body open to the sky and rain.

## Shakti Resort, Leti, Uttaranchal, 2007

The resort is a series of small guest units, some protruding from, and others literally carved into, the landscape following the contours of the foothills of the Himalayas, at 2,500 metres (8,202 feet), in northern India. The project is a passive reworking of the landscape through gathering, moving and condensing native materials into cohesive but temporary structures that do not attempt to challenge the transformative effects of time. Half-metre (1.6-foot) thick stone walls provide weight and texture to each structure while glazed surfaces, oriented outwards, visually connect the occupants with mountains, distant glaciers, white peaks, hawks and eagles in flight, constantly shifting cloud formations, sunrises, sunsets and starry skies.

## Jamshyd Sethna House, Nandgaon, Alibag, Maharashtra, 2004–

Situated in a coconut palm and betelnut grove on a remote section of coastline south of Mumbai, the house is designed as a place for refuge, and is made up of spaces that shelter from, as well as invite in, the elements, mediating and regulating air, water and light. Three volumes, two above ground and one below, slide into, and are set within, the coconut grove, looking out to infinite horizons in all directions – the ocean in one and a seemingly endless density of coconut trunks in the other. The built structures echo the site with its coconut-palm trunks rising vertically like columns to support an almost continuous canopy of palm leaves.

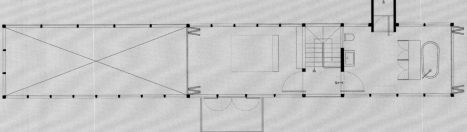

## Reading Room addition, Nandgaon, Alibag, 2003

This small addition to an existing house, located 60 kilometres (37 miles) south of Mumbai on the western coast, is nestled under the shade of a large banyan tree. Using the traditional building techniques of the area, the structure is made from recycled Burma teak wood which is knitted to the main part of the house. The walls of the addition are translucent, wrapped in a white permeable screen that admits gentle breezes and dappled light during the day.

## Nikhil Kapoor House, Kashid, Murud, 2003

Nestled in a forested valley across the bay from Mumbai, the Nikhil Kapoor House functions like a large covered verandah, in which one is simultaneously indoors and outdoors, cooled by the breeze and sheltered from the sun and rain. Creeping vines blanket the black-basalt rubble masonry of the north facade. Solid on one side, and open on the other, living spaces physically extend out into the garden while the forest is visually invited to the doorstep.

## Nilofer Kapadia House, Satirje, Alibag, 2004

Located in the midst of an arid rural landscape south of Mumbai, the house is planned to be lived in and around, its semisheltered and open-air spaces integrated within the structure in a way that invites flexible uses and an interaction with garden, sky and weather. A 'secret garden' weaves around the perimeter, augmenting and defining semiprivate sleeping and bathing areas. An outer wall acts not so much as a fence, but as the outermost surface of the house itself, so that courtyards, gardens, trees, vines and soil are as integral to the everyday living spaces as the floors, walls and furniture. Four separate stairways lead to a series of roof pavilions, some uncovered and some enclosed. A lounge, a bedroom, an open sleeping porch and several window boxes act as private but interconnected tree-top nests, allowing the ceiling to extend to the sky and the tree-tops to form an aerial botanical landscape.

Text © 2007 John Wiley & Sons Ltd. Images: pp 36–39, 40(r), 41 © Studio Mumbai Architects; p 40(l) © Studio Mumbai Architects, photo Michael Freeman

# Rahul Mehrotra Associates

Rahul Mehrotra maintains a diverse and active role as an architect, urban activist, writer and teacher. His book *Bombay: The Cities Within* (1995), with Sharada Dwivedi, is a major enquiry into the history and sociology of India's vivacious and contentious urbanism. He finds his city of practice – Mumbai – a mine for quarrying architectural ideations and languages. Unlike most regions in India that may have to adhere to a conformist cultural agenda, Mumbai offers a conceptual freedom in traversing the traditional and contemporary as the city has its particular plurality in the intertwining epochs, attitudes and 'coming together and moving apart of the past and present'. Multiplicity is thus axiomatic in Mehrotra's interpretation of the city, although this is transferred in his architecture as a dialogical juxtaposition of public and private, exteriority and interiority, natural and industrial materials, and the traditional and contemporary.

Interiority, arising both from reasons of climate and urban conditions, is an abiding theme in Mehrotra's work and is articulated through reified courtyards and walls that also retain an intimate conversation with the larger landscape. From residences to large complexes, he uses these elements with great craft and finesse to create dramatic spaces with changing palettes of materials, colours and phenomenally modulated differences between the exterior and interior.

'In our projects, the approach has been to abstract and interpret spatial arrangements as well as building vocabulary,' he says. 'The idea is to combine materials, to juxtapose conventional craftsmanship with industrial materials and traditional spatial arrangements with contemporary space organisation. In short, to give expression to the multiple worlds, pluralism and dualities that so vividly characterise the Asian landscape.'

## Corner Plot House, Chennai, 2003–

The house is designed around a courtyard, creating a sense of privacy that a corner plot would not otherwise offer. The courtyard contains a pool that penetrates through the house and culminates in an area at the end of the court used for performance. The spaces around the courtyard are transparent, creating a complete blur between inside and out. The terrace is designed as a landscape and includes an amphitheatre, garden, lotus pond and a meditation space. The rich palette of materials used for the exterior offsets the austere quality of the internal spaces.

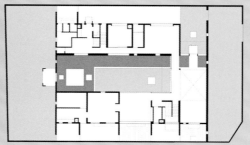

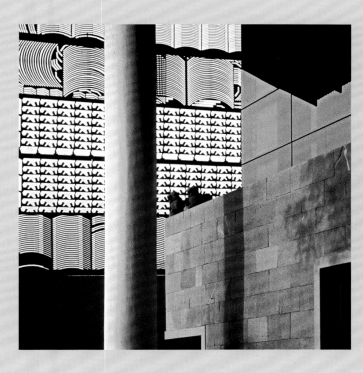

## Rural Campus for Tata Institute of Social Sciences (TISS), Tuljapur, Maharashtra, 2004

The campus is located in Tuljapur in the hinterland of the state of Maharashtra. The programmes at the institution involve development issues ranging from social forestry to health and infrastructure. Responding to this agenda and the organisation patterns in the region, the layout of the campus is formed by a series of buildings clustered around courtyards, which creates an interesting range of open and covered spaces. These spaces facilitate social interaction and multiple uses, and provide wonderful gathering areas in the evenings or in cool weather.

In response to the local conditions, the use of appropriate building materials was explored and the buildings were constructed using local stone for load-bearing walls, and an inexpensive and innovative ferrocement vault for the roofing system. In addition, wind towers, a precedent from the locale, were introduced in all buildings to integrate passive cooling for the interior spaces.

## House for a Film Maker, Alibag, 2001

This weekend retreat for a film maker and his family is situated on a 0.4-hectare (1-acre) plot in the village of Kihim in the Alibag district (across the harbour from Mumbai city). The location of the house divides the plot into two distinct zones: one of predominantly teak trees and the other accommodating a manicured garden. The living room (which is literally a large verandah space) opens on to the teak zone while the bedrooms overlook the garden area. This zoning of the site also creates a distinct public and private face to the house, which is expressed in the finish and levels of transparency in the different spaces. The spatial layout of the house is organised by a linear spine that amplifies the duality. Small courtyards interspersed in the central spine create a dramatic modulation of light in the spinal space.

The central spine is covered with a low reinforced-cement concrete slab on which rests the roof, a light metal frame clad in galvanised iron sheets. The walls are built in local stone, rooting the building to the context, while the light metal-clad roof sits gently on this base, creating a visual juxtaposition of local and industrial materials as well as traditional and modern technologies.

The interior of the house is richer in texture with a palette of finishes including natural stone for the floor, bare concrete, and wooden platforms and walls with patinas.

## House on an Orchard, near Ahmedabad, 2004

Located in the middle of an 8-hectare (20-acre) mango orchard, this single-family weekend retreat is organised with a courtyard as the focus of the house. Because of the hot dry climate of Ahmedabad, the house was located in the centre of an orchard rather than on the edge of the site. It is conceived as an oasis that is arrived at after meandering through the orchard. Besides being a naturally insulated location, the green cover also serves as a visual relief in the summer months when the acute glare from the sun can be very uncomfortable. The terrace is a landscape feature with seating platforms and pavilions facilitating its use in the evenings when the temperature drops sharply, compared to the interior which takes longer to become cool.

The outer skin of the house is made of local Porbunder sandstone, which emphasises the textures of a semidesert landscape. On entering through this external skin, the sight of the water in the courtyard and the plastered surfaces with their various vibrant colours create a feeling of instant relief. The blue colour of the water in the pool is folded over an adjoining wall, exaggerating the presence of water and enhancing the contrast between inside and out. In addition, the courtyard accommodates a swimming pool filled with fresh water that is used to recharge the wells on the property when the house is closed after its use at the weekend.

## Laxmi Machine Works (LMW) corporate office, Coimbatore, Tamil Nadu, 1998

The building was designed to house the Laxmi Machine Works' eight subsidiaries within a collective identity, yet allowing for separate entrances. Given the location of the site, off the main commercial street of the city, sandwiched between industrial establishments along one edge and the army cantonment on the other side, the design response was a low-rise building with a large footprint that respects the surrounding fabric.

The works are constructed around three courtyards varying in scale and use. The entrance courtyard is the most public, from which one ascends to the more secluded inner courtyards. The spaces provide a vista through the building, establishing the idea of centrality and a clear axis along which the various components of the building are organised. Water in the inner courtyards is circulated to humidify the spaces – an ideal device for the hot, dry climate of Coimbatore, which lies in the rain-shadow of the Nilgiri Hills. Cross-ventilation and air circulation, coupled with the humidification of air, cools the building very efficiently.

Artist Yogesh Rawal, in collaboration with Rajeev Sethi, used scrap metal to create an array of screens and trellises that not only secure the building but also facilitate the movement of air and light. One of the largest manufacturers of machine tools, the client provided an enormous source for the scrap metal.

## Restoration of Chowmahalla Palace, Hyderabad, 2002–

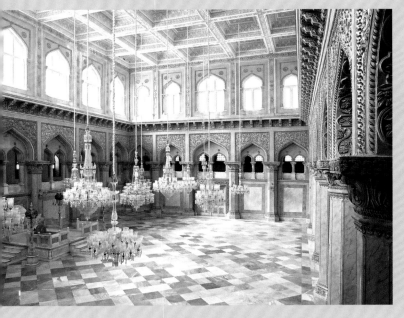

The Chowmahalla Palace was built by Nizam Salabat Jung in the 1750s as one of the first examples of European neoclassical architecture in Hyderabad. The complex, which consists of buildings around two main courtyards, grew incrementally over the years, thus displaying consistencies in its architectural styles. It has two clear parts: the first is a series of rooms around a large courtyard and water body within the main Khilwat (the centrepiece of the complex) located at the apex of the courtyard. The rooms have now been adapted as spaces for craftspeople to work in and from which to sell their wares. The Khilwat, containing the Darbar Hall (Throne Room), is being restored and converted into a museum of costumes and artefacts from the Nizam collection. The second half of the complex contains four palaces, also organised around a courtyard and water body, which will be restored to create museums of the Nizam dynasty.

Urban densification around the palace, illegal encroachments and prolonged disuse caused major deterioration in many of the buildings. The restoration was carried out using traditional craftspeople and techniques, and a range of elements was conserved in order to maintain the integrity of these historic structures.

Text © 2007 John Wiley & Sons Ltd. Images: p 42 © courtesy Rahul Mehrotra; p 43(t), 44, 45(b) © RMA, photos Rajesh Vora; p 43(b), 45(t) © RMA, photos Rahul Mehrotra

# Samira Rathod Design Associates

Tectonic and delightful, the work of Samira Rathod displays an exacting sense of materiality, tactility and crafting combined with playful experimentation and innovation. Rathod joins a new group of Indian architects who do not lean towards the representational repertoire of signs and symbols, but rather towards the sheer delight of presence where material juxtaposition and phenomenal fabrication speak for themselves. Deeply involved in the design and production of furniture (she once ran a furniture store called Tranceforme), Rathod carries that sensibility into architecture in an instrumental and conceptual manner. Site and the affective conditions of the landscape are also important progenitors of her architecture.

Whether it is a tree house made of canvas and gunny bags, a maze in a forest made of wooden logs, a high-end store whose spaces are continuously re-created by repositionable panels of rich fabric hung from steel tracks, or a door of 2-tonne concrete, Rathod is a consummate materialist in the most poetic sense. On each occasion there is always a subtle turn towards what she describes as 'a trance, a mood that brings sheer delight'.

## Karjat Farmhouse, Karjat, Maharashtra, 2001

On a site that attracts migratory birds, it was important that the house blend into the environment so as to keep the birds from leaving. As a result, an existing row of trees was left undisturbed and the spaces of the understated house conceived around them, on top of a large mound resting 4.2 metres (14 feet) above a man-made lake.

## Interactive Maze, Colaba Woods, Mumbai, 2002

This installation for the city of Mumbai, designed in the city's wooded area, was inspired by the wood itself. A maze made out of red and blue wooden logs challenges children to find their way to its core, and back out again.

## Palete, Mahalaxmi, Mumbai, 2004

Designed as a highly flexible fabric and lifestyle store of 650 square metres (7,000 square feet), the ceiling is marked with a steel grid of tracks that allows about 150 panels to be moved and positioned to create different kinds of areas within the overall space. Another special feature is the 2-tonne concrete entrance door.

## Office interiors for Asian Age, Mumbai, 2002

This modern office environment for a newspaper agency is literally inserted into an existing printing shed. The intervention lies within the first 3 metres (10 feet) of space, allowing the old shed to be visible in the new office space. An interesting play of new and conventional materials is juxtaposed with the existing old brick and trusses above.

## Tree House, Bharuch, Gujarat, 2000

Created for young teenagers to see in the new millennium atop a tree, this playhouse is made from canvas, gunny bags and eucalyptus-tree logs. At 56 square metres (600 square feet), it is perched as three boxes under a large rain tree.

## Kishore Mariwala House, Alibag, 2006

The house was designed for a couple as the further evolution of two previous houses, and is a spatial narrative and material ensemble. Three forms are connected by a spine, with each form representing a different mood and condition. The house exudes a sense of exuberance and fun in a coherent manner in which the three incongruous forms are amalgamated to create the living spaces. Rathod's idea of design as conducting a musical composition is reflected in the symphonic (more jazz-like) nature of the whole ensemble.

Text © 2007 John Wiley & Sons Ltd. Images: p 46 © SRDA, photos Rajeshwar; p 47(t) © SRDA, photo Samira Rathod; p 47(b) SRDA, photos Sebastian Zachariah; p 48(t) © SRDA, photos Mr Nrupen Madhvani; p 48(b) © SRDA, photos Samira Rathod; p 49 © SRDA, photos David D'Souza

# Auroville
## An Architectural Laboratory

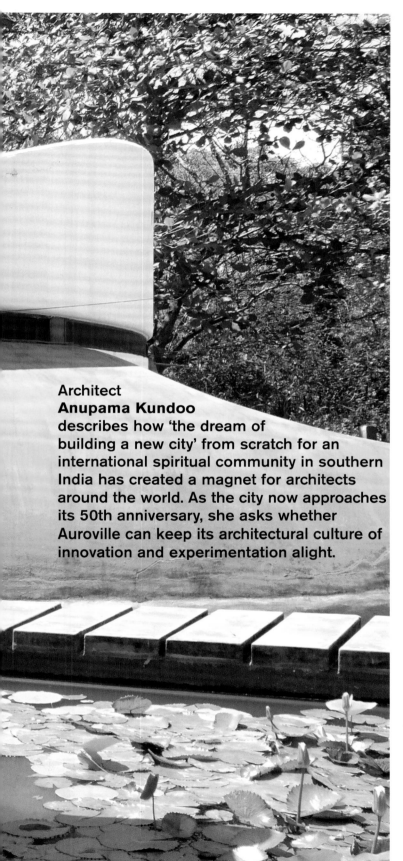

Architect
**Anupama Kundoo**
describes how 'the dream of building a new city' from scratch for an international spiritual community in southern India has created a magnet for architects around the world. As the city now approaches its 50th anniversary, she asks whether Auroville can keep its architectural culture of innovation and experimentation alight.

More than a decade before Le Corbusier and Louis Kahn arrived on the Indian architectural scene, India's first example of Modern architecture, built prior to independence, was being realised in a small pocket of French India, Pondicherry, 150 kilometres (93 miles) south of Chennai, in 1938. The spiritual leader Sri Aurobindo Ghose and his spiritual partner Mirra Alfassa, better known as the Mother,[1] envisioned a state-of-the-art dormitory for the members of their rapidly expanding ashram, and invited Antonin Raymond, a former disciple of Frank Lloyd Wright, to design the project. The result was Golconde, India's first reinforced-concrete building, which achieved a standard that is hard to reach even today.

**The Vision of a City**

Thirty years later, in 1968, the Mother envisioned a new city, Auroville, named after Sri Aurobindo, dedicated to achieving human unity and international understanding. Auroville was inaugurated 10 kilometres (6.2 miles) north of Pondicherry on a barren wasteland with the participation of 5,000 people from 125 countries and all Indian states, each of whom brought a handful of earth from their homeland to a marble-clad lotus-bud shaped urn that still stands at the centre of this planned city. The Mother invited French architect Roger Anger to design this project. Of the several concepts for the proposed city of 50,000 inhabitants, the one selected became popularly known as the 'galaxy concept'. It housed four zones – Residential, Industrial, Cultural and International – in a radiating but dynamic spirally rotated movement around the city centre, consisting of a lake, parks and gardens, and the Matrimandir, a central structure representing the soul of the city and a space for concentration.

Being compact, at only 2.5 kilometres (1.5 miles) in diameter, the city offers ease of mobility. A concentric road called the Crown, located midway, at once became the main traffic distributor cutting through all the zones while housing the prominent public buildings to service each zone. This keeps the city centre, the area contained within this road, free of congestion and means the town resembles a garden city.

The dream of building a new city for the future on a 'clean slate', with the purpose of promoting research and experimentation alongside integral development, has been attracting architects and students from all over the world ever since Auroville's inception. Without predefined bylaws or being bound by the conventions of human society, a multitude of expressions materialised in the course of Auroville's development.

**Roger Anger, Aster's House, Auromodele, Auroville, 1971**
The first of the houses in Auromodele – a settlement planned at the outskirts of Auroville as an experiment in how to live in the new city. A huge cast-in-situ ferrocement, double-curved roof extends the potential of the material and initiates a series of further expressions. At a time when there was no vegetation, the earth berms were seen as a continuation of the red earth landscape.

**Antonin Raymond, Golconde, Pondicherry, Tamil Nadu, 1945**
India's first example of Modern architecture and of the first use of reinforced cement concrete commissioned by the founders of Auroville, continues to serve as a bench mark for the high standard of architecture aspired to at the time. The building still stands as one of the best examples of climatic comfort through passive cooling, its entire facade composed of custom-made prefabricated operable asbestos louvres to let in the southeast breeze.

**Roger Anger, Concept for the city of Auroville, Tamil Nadu, 1968**
For 50,000 citizens in a compact area 2.5 kilometres (1.5 miles) in diameter, the plan contains four zones – Residential, Cultural, Industrial and International – that radiate around a central green space in a dynamic spiral. A green belt of around 1.25 kilometres (0.75 miles) is planned around the city proper.

## Pioneers and Subsequent Developments

The aim of Auroville, as declared in its charter, to be a 'site of material and spiritual researches', was addressed by its pioneer settlers in a number of different ways.

Roger Anger had kick-started the experimental spirit through his earliest projects. His early houses in Auromodele on the outskirts of the city, and school buildings in Aspiration, demonstrated exemplary innovations at various levels, from the programme to the forms and building technologies, creating the precedence and inspiration for extensive applied research in architecture. Architects and various architectural aspirants from all over the world, as well as neighbouring cities and villages, who were absorbed into Anger's office, recall the high concentration of creative energy and collective work in those early days when the excitement of this idealistic project was still fresh and the Mother was still available for regular reviews and discussions. Matrimandir, on which Anger continues to work, will be inaugurated this year.

Piero and Gloria Cicionesi, an architect couple from Italy, were in Auroville from almost the beginning and realised some of its outstanding architectural projects. Among the first houses to be built in Auroville, Auroson's Home (1969–70) is an example of excellence and elegance. Another notable project was the community housing in Aspiration, with its community kitchen that served as a hub for years.

**Roger Anger, Last School, Auroville, 1971**
This sculptural piece of architecture is noted for its modular roofing elements assembled over large storm-water drains that also serve as structural beams.

Though planned as temporary housing, the Aspiration, development is still today among the most successful (although it is not well maintained), and accommodates a wide variety of Aurovilians. The Cicionesis also produced a palette of school buildings in the Transition campus, the latest addition to which is the Future School building (2003). Greatly inspired by Golconde, the Italian couple strive towards 'sober, honest, simple, elegant and wise' design solutions. Piero led the construction work of Matrimandir for 12 years and was responsible for making possible the participation of unskilled community members.

Poppo Pingel, another pioneering architect, arrived in Auroville in 1970 with an initial social preoccupation around experimental village housing. This led to several innovative

**Roger Anger, Sanskrit School, Auroville, 1971**
Here, free-flowing spaces held by free-flowing playful forms were realised while experimenting with ferrocement technology that permits almost any shape.

**Bhagwandas, Dome House, Auroville, 1973**
The Dome House is one of several adventurous experiments in housing undertaken in the pioneering days, not only in terms of building technology but also in terms of lifestyle and programme. The mobile roof could be rotated according to the season and time of day.

**Poppo Pingel, Fraternity Workshops, Auroville, 1971**
An investigation into the potential of asbestos roofing sheets in other parts of the structure, the facade here can be completely opened by operating the large panels connected as a vertical system of louvres.

projects in rammed earth and the creation of outstanding workshops. In the late 1970s Pingel built a series of residential buildings using arches, vaults and domes in response to the emerging energy crisis. More recently his focus has moved to 'baubiology' (the impact of buildings on human health in an integral sense). Calling archaeology 'reverse architecture', he has over the years conducted archaeological 'rescue' excavations mainly out of the foundation pits of new projects, and extracted enough valuable material to fill a little museum.

Pingel was the first to receive students for practical training in architecture in 1985, little knowing that he was starting a trend. Suhasini Ayer-Guigan and Lata Iyer were his first students, and eventually settled in Auroville. Suhasini went on to build an enormous number of projects all over Auroville, including the Solar Kitchen.

Ajit Koujalgi, who earlier worked in Anger's office, has shifted his focus to 'finding a timeless architecture' and is mainly preoccupied with architectural conservation. Helmut Schmid, largely inspired by Kahn, has built several exposed-brick buildings in Auroville, although his projects in Pondicherry, particularly his Skyline apartments, are probably

his more excellent work. Health Centre Staff Quarters and more recently Savitri Bhavan are his better-known public buildings in Auroville.

Meanwhile, in the informal development of Auroville, semi-permanent structures in casuarinas roundwood and coconut-rope joinery thatched with coconut-leaf mats became the vocabulary, enabling settlers to steward the widespread lands at a low price. John Allen, an Australian architect, developed the 'capsule', the smallest stable dwelling unit still popularly used.

One has also seen in Auroville a whole range of exciting experiments undertaken by non-architects, such as Bhagwandas' Dome House, though unfortunately many of these no longer exist. The quest for alternative technologies bore abundant fruits. People built on the experiments of others and took technological innovations further, as seen in the evolution of the ferrocement technology that almost became a household affair in the surrounding villages. More formally, high-quality prefabricated ferrocement components, including biogas plants and water tanks, were made available at the Center for Scientific Research led by Tency Beatens.

**Roger Anger, Matrimandir, Auroville, 1971–2007**
Matrimandir, a space for concentration, is located at the centre of the city.

**Fabian Ostner, House for Klara, Auroville, 2003**
A hybrid and structurally challenging building, this house attempts to create interesting and aesthetic living spaces within a flexible steel structure using industrial materials not commonly found in India's residential architecture.

From 1985 Ray Meeker, an American ceramist, experimented with fire-stabilised mud houses. Over 20 years he built 20 projects, systematically furthering the technique of building mud houses, filling them as kilns, and cooking both products and the kiln-cum-house in one go. Agnijata (1990), his first big house, is still very much in use.

Younger architects like Mona Doctor-Pingel, Satprem Maini and myself arrived in Auroville at the end of the 1980s.

Maini, a postgraduate in earth architecture from Grenoble, created a state-of-the-art technical laboratory for earth construction analysis. He set up the Earth Unit, Auroville Building Center, and provides consultancy and training to architects and students as well as working on his own projects in several countries. Noteworthy amongst the work of architects who settled in subsequent years are Dominique Dube's House for Inge and first units of Progress, David Nightingale and Ganesh Bala's Integral Learning Center, Fabian Ostner's House for Klara and Jana Dreikhausen's own residence.

### The Challenge of Remaining a Laboratory

The pioneering years definitely witnessed a rich variety of experiments in form, building materials and construction technologies. One wonders whether things have slowed down now as older architects whose earlier works overflowed with innovations have become more settled in their approach. Or, are the clients now less pioneering too, wishing to take fewer risks and having more conventional lifestyles? Pingel explains this phenomenon as innovation having been a necessity in a new situation where nothing was available, where there was a severe lack of locally available industrial materials or skilled masons and carpenters. They weren't inventing for its own sake, but in order to find solutions to problems that now are unnecessary.

For Anger, experimentation and innovation must remain an integral part of Auroville's architecture, and a high standard of architecture must always be aspired to. The Mother is said to have declared: 'Auroville wants to be a field of constant research for architectural expressions, manifesting a new spirit through new forms.'

Auroville is now better known for its sustainable building examples. In the course of its success in reforestation, renewable technologies and eco-building alternatives engaged in by the community at large, the last two decades have seen a quest for sustainable and low-cost alternatives to building and less of the excitement of architectural expressions of earlier times. Auroville also offers itself as a 'laboratory' for

**Helmut Schmid, House for Surendra Gupta, Pondicherry, 1992**
Schmid has designed several housing apartments in Pondicherry, bringing high-quality design and construction into the mainstream.

**David Nightingale and Ganesh Bala, Integral Learning Center, Auroville, 2006**
A rammed-earth wall enclosing the compound and terminating at the entrance creates visual privacy while the changing and storage facilities provide the necessary closure towards the rear. A space of quiet introspection forms the backdrop for a wide variety of workshops and the culturally diverse groups who use the building.

**Ivana Bocina and students of the Architectural Association (London), Enormous Eyrie, Auroville, 2007**
This watchtower for schoolchildren, designed and built in the botanical gardens by students of the AA, was part of a workshop exploring 1:1 model-making as a design tool.

students of architecture from elsewhere, who participate in the various workshops here. Students from the University of Washington, Seattle, recently built a dormitory in rammed earth. This year, under my guidance, students of the Architectural Association in London designed and built a watchtower in the botanical gardens.

With the rapid urbanisation of every little town, Auroville can no longer entertain the illusion of the present paradise-like, low-density community life. As a response, its master plan has seen a new awakening, as a possible tool to protect the project but also to take it further towards its aim of becoming a city, thereby accelerating the slow rate of development of recent years. It is hoped that, if Aurovilians manage to go beyond the internal polarities between developing and remaining nostalgic, this master plan could unblock a whole range of other projects that Auroville might be ready for. If simultaneously Auroville could revamp its administrative structure, which evolved for the governance of a handful of people, into a more open one that can once again open its doors to newcomers, the experiment could see fresh young blood and a reawakening of the spirit.

Clearly a change is at the threshold. An urban life, a city life as opposed to widespread decentralised communities, and a whole new range of architectural expressions can once again take shape, welcoming new architects from all over the world without fear, as in the days following the town's inauguration. With the International zone becoming more active and Auroville moving towards its own goal of becoming a city, it could begin again to attract people for its original purpose, rather than new-age tourists and the like.

All in all, nearly 40 years on, the significant number and variety of projects in Auroville need to be analysed in terms of replicability and relevance, not only for the further development of Auroville, but also, probably, for the rest of India and the world. ⚿

**Note**
1. After a short political career in which Aurobindo Ghose (1872–1950) became one of India's leading freedom fighters, Sri Aurobindo – as he was later called – turned to spiritual life, the practice of a new spiritual path, the 'integral yoga', the aim of which was to further the evolution of life on earth. Sri Aurobindo wrote extensively in English on his spiritual philosophy and practice as well as on social and political development, Indian culture, literature and poetry. He also wrote poetry. His spiritual partner was the Mother (1878–1973). Mirra Alfassa – as she was known before she came to India – was born in Paris to Turkish and Egyptian parents, and finally settled in Pondicherry in 1920 after several visits to Sri Aurobindo's ashram. She supervised the organisation of his ashram and related institutions after Sri Aurobindo retired into seclusion in 1926 and led the community after his death in 1950.

Text © 2007 John Wiley & Sons Ltd. Images: pp 50-1, 54(tl), 55(b) © Anne Pind; pp 52(tl), 53(t) © Anupama Kundoo; pp 52(tr&b), 53(bl&r) © Dominique Darr; p 54(tr) © John Mandeen; p 54(b) © Andreas Deffner; p 55(t) © Ireno Guerci

# Local Stone (A Fragment)

At a time when a wide range of building materials is available around the world, the decision to use locally sourced stone in India often extends beyond the pragmatic. As **Reinhold Martin** explains, a particular choice of stone can potentially set off a complex string of associations with geopolitical connotations.

**Charles Correa, Life Insurance Corporation of India (LIC) Building, New Delhi, 1986**
Locally quarried red sandstone is here juxtaposed with commercially available mirrored glass.

Often enough, construction materials serve as a locus of political or proto-political fantasy. Think, for example, of the emancipatory potential attached to glass and steel throughout the 20th century, right up to the politics of transparency surrounding Norman Foster's 'reconstruction' of Berlin's Reichstag in 1999. But less frequently is a construction material capable of sustaining what is, in effect, a doubled-up form of *geo*politics, in the sense of a politics informed by both geography and geology. Such is the case with what is called, in the idiom of professional architects, 'local stone'. In many different ways the geological history of a site or geographic region and, along with it, the potential use of a locally available resource like stone in the construction of a building can be interpolated into complex strings of imaginative associations. Within such concatenations, 'local' should not necessarily be thought of as opposed to 'global' and all that this word signals in today's debates over so-called globalisation. Instead, in the case of contemporary architecture, 'local' and 'global' work more frequently as quasi-synonyms rather than as antonyms. And architecture in India – or really, 'India' – is no exception.

Rethinking the terms under which today's globalisation debates are conducted requires guidance from history. In India, as in many other countries in the global South, 'local' has for some time now indicated opposition to the universalising norms of Modernist aesthetics or to certain aspects of post-independence modernisation policy, or both. And so, as in related strategies of opposition mounted in the North, what makes 'local stone' local is its capacity to index technical processes and to stage aesthetic effects that seem to bind a particular building to a particular place and thereby (presumably) render it unsusceptible to modernity's deracinating abstractions. In India today we might explore this assumption by taking up the use of local grey granite by Sanjay Mohe in his respectful 2003 addition to Balkrishna V

Typical commercial building with sandstone cladding, under construction in Gurgaon around 2003.

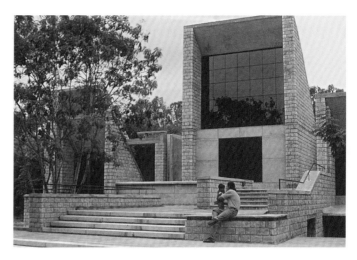

**Sanjay Mohe, GIV Building, Bangalore, 2003**
Locally quarried grey granite is used in both the original complex and in this recent addition to the Balkrishna V Doshi Indian Institute of Management of 1985.

Doshi's 1985 Indian Institute of Management (IIM) in Bangalore. Or we might consider the sporadic use of sandstone cladding in commercial buildings like those recently constructed in Gurgaon. On their surfaces, these two recent examples may seem to have opposite consequences. In the case of Mohe's addition to Doshi's campus, the stone comes from the ground, as it were, and can therefore be imagined to anchor the building to its site. Whereas in Gurgaon's commercial architecture, stone – still coming from the local ground – seems just as uprooted and de-ontologised, just as much an off-the-shelf product (visible in roadside clearinghouses, in this case) as the glass against which it is juxtaposed. In light of such tensions, and at the risk of allowing the overdetermined part to stand in for the fictional whole, we shall restrict ourselves to reconstructing a tiny fragment of this story by way of two buildings realised by Charles Correa in the 1980s and early 1990s.

At around the same time that architectonic citations of 'vernacular' or classical (that is, Western monumental) traditions were beginning to dominate in the US and Europe, both Correa and Raj Rewal began cladding public buildings in sandstone quarried in the area around Delhi. In doing so they were helping to define a Postmodernism whose own foundation myths locate its origins in Euro-America. Early in their respective careers, both had undertaken exercises in exposed or painted reinforced concrete – Correa with his very own Lever House, an exhibition pavilion designed for Hindustan Lever in 1961, and Rewal for a pair of much larger pavilions for the International Trade Fair in New Delhi (1972). In 1980 Correa had also built the 21-storey Visvesvaraya Centre in Bangalore, developed by the state-owned Life Insurance Corporation of India (LIC) – a set of raw concrete towers topped with periscopic heads. But when faced with another high-rise commission for the same client on New Delhi's Connaught Place, begun in 1975 and completed in 1986, Correa clad the

**Herbert Baker, Secretariat, New Delhi, 1930**
This project used locally quarried red and beige sandstone throughout, in a 'contextual' reference.

**Fatehpur Sikri, Agra, c 1569**
Detail. A major monument from the Mogul period, the Fatehpur Sikri is executed in locally quarried red sandstone throughout.

resulting pair of quasi-triangular towers in the red sandstone typically quarried in the Delhi area or in neighbouring Rajasthan, set off against expanses of mirrored glass.

Why? Rather than refer to the 'properly' neoclassical facades of Connaught Place, executed in white-painted stucco, Correa seemingly chose to confront New Delhi, planned and built by the British Raj, with an earlier imperial episode in the history of the Indian subcontinent, the reign of the Mogul princes that began in the 16th century. He did so through the use of stone and, in a sense, through stone alone. But there was nothing ontologically 'local' or (what amounts to the same thing here) 'prehistorical' about the stone that Correa used, since it had already become an element and an image circulating within geopolitical discourse, with the help of Edwin Lutyens and Herbert Baker in the Viceroy's House, the Secretariat, and other monuments in imperial New Delhi. In response to official requests that their architecture 'appeal to Orientals as well as to Europeans',[1] Lutyens, Baker and others responsible for the architecture of New Delhi had intermittent (if reluctant) recourse to motifs drawn from the Indo-Saracenic architecture codified during the 19th century by Orientalists like James Fergusson and Swinton Jacob. This style was predominantly associated with monuments of the Mogul period such as the 16th-century imperial compound of Fatehpur Sikri. Thus the New Delhi complex combined *chattris* (pavilions), *jhallis* (carved stone screens) and other Indo-Saracenic elements with the colonnades, flanking symmetries and hemispherical domes of European neoclassicism. But more importantly for our purposes here, these monuments were clad in the red and beige sandstone quarried from the surrounding region, also to be found in abundance at Fatehpur Sikri, the Red Fort at Agra and other monuments from the Mogul period.

So Correa's citation in stone at LIC New Delhi can be reconstructed as follows: the red sandstone used there, adjacent to the starkly neoclassical, stucco-clad monumentality of Connaught Place (and, not incidentally, within sight of the Jantar Mantar observatory, awash in deep reds), quoted the early 20th-century British imperium as it, in turn, quoted the 16th-century Mogul imperium both to

consolidate and to dissimulate its own imperial status. Read geopolitically, however, the order of citation should really be reversed to yield a counter-chronology that reflects the Postmodern order of things in the early 1980s in India. In such a sequence, red sandstone is first associated with the (earlier) Mogul monuments and only secondarily with the (later) British ones. This reversal can be seen as critical, since in referring to Mogul architecture, it deflects both the neoclassical monumentality of Connaught Place (associated with the British), and the Hindu-centric nativism implicit in the ideologies of 'Indianness' that had, by then, begun to replace 'Oriental' as a signifier of difference from Euro-American architectural styles. But by appealing subliminally to an ontologically 'raw', unmediated geology (set in contrast to the imagistic commercialism of mirrored glass, demineralised) it actively forgets, rather than complicates, the more recent assimilation of that same Mogul architecture and its stone into an essentialist imperial narrative in the hands of Lutyens and Baker.

This doubling up of geopolitics, in the form of incommensurable territorial claims rendered in stone, is effaced as red sandstone works in a number of subsequent buildings executed by Correa to establish something like a regularity of statements. This occurs most obviously at the level of what is said (and what is not said) about the buildings themselves. The signal instance of such a pattern is Correa's Jawahar Kala Kendra, a multipurpose cultural centre in Jaipur (in Rajasthan) dedicated to the memory of Jawaharlal Nehru, begun in 1986 and completed in 1992. Again and again, accounts of the building do not fail to note the 'local' provenance of the building's red sandstone cladding. This generally occurs by way of reference to Mogul monuments, while consistently omitting any reference to the New Delhi of Lutyens and Baker.

Here are a few excerpts:

*The external walls ... are clad in sandstone (from Rajasthan) with a coping of beige Dholpur stone – the same material used for the Jantar Mantar Observatory [in Jaipur], Fatehpur Sikri and the Red Fort at Agra.*
— 'In focus: Charles Correa', *Architecture + Design*, 1991[2]

**Charles Correa, Jawahar Kala Kendra, Jaipur, 1992**
Another example of the use of local red sandstone.

*The exterior, comprising tall blank walls – pierced only here and there by a few square openings – and clothed in large slabs of the beautiful, local, crimson red sandstone, is like Charles's personal signature on a work of art.*
— Satish Grover, 'Charles Correa: A view from Delhi', *Architecture + Design*, 1991[3]

*The external walls of the buildings (including those around the central kund) are clad in red Agra sandstone, topped by a coping of beige Dholpur stone – the same materials used for the Jantar Mantar Observatory, in the Red Fort at Agra, and in Fatehpur Sikri.*
— Image caption in Charles Correa, *Charles Correa*, 1996[4]

*The implicitly regional character of this institution finds expression in the red Rajasthan sandstone with which it is faced, topped by copings of beige Dholpur stone. These are the same materials that were used for the Jantar Mantar Observatory at Fatehpur Sikri [sic] and in the Red Fort at Agra.*
— Kenneth Frampton, 'The work of Charles Correa', in *Charles Correa*, 1996[5]

At one level such repetition is no doubt a tribute to Frampton's own arguments in 'Towards a Critical Regionalism' (1983) in favour of an architecture that 'builds' its site by inscribing 'its history in both a geological and agricultural sense'.[6] Though taken a bit more literally by architects like Correa than Frampton's complex sense of the tectonic might otherwise allow, it nevertheless represents an effort to resist the onslaught of homogeneity to which a more geographically neutral (that is, more classically Modernist) idiom might be vulnerable. Still, our own sense of geopolitical incommensurability is heightened when we consider that, in the deployment of 'local stone' in Correa's work, this resistance is mounted at the level of only apparently stable representations – in other words, as ideology – rather than at

the level of discourse itself. For at a properly discursive level, 'local/global' organises the field of possible statements immanent to the discursive formation – and indeed, the practices – that we name with such vague terms as globalisation (or, in the case of an important target of Frampton's original argument, Postmodernism). In other words, at the discursive level there is nothing more global than 'local stone'.

This characterisation of a construction material as discursively constructed poses distinct interpretative problems. These are compounded with respect to a building such as the Jawahar Kala Kendra, for which 'mythology' consultants were employed to assist in formulating the symbolic narratives that informed its nine-square mandala plan, which is based on the Vedic *shastras* (sacred writings).[7] Despite the emphasis on iconography that such practices encourage, it is important that we adjust our notion of discourse to take in the actual (and in many ways, non-verbal) constructedness of materials themselves, not as simulacra but as hybrids – in this case, irreducibly competing and contested admixtures of geology, geography and politics. In this small fragment excerpted from Correa's work, 'local stone' thus stages a form of geopolitics in which the quasi-secular (as opposed to the militantly Hindu) construction 'Indian' is substituted for two sides of Modernism: international and British/imperial. That this particular geopolitics is inherently resistant to, rather than complicit with, the neo-Orientalist, neo-imperial reflex in which European, American *and* Indian architects regularly participate today is, perhaps, a myth more impervious than the stone itself. ∆

This text elaborates on material explored in collaboration with Kadambari Baxi in *Multi-National City: Architectural Itineraries*, Actar (Barcelona), 2007. I am also grateful to Pradeep Dalal for his insights on the subject.

Notes
1. Viceroy of India Lord Hardinge to former viceroy Lord Curzon, 22 October 1912, quoted in Thomas R Metcalf, *An Imperial Vision: Indian Architecture and Britain's Raj*, University of California Press (Berkeley, CA), 1989, p 219. In a chapter dedicated to the architecture of the new capital, Metcalf documents the stylistic debates among British administrators and the architects and planners of New Delhi. On the politics informing the design of New Delhi, see also Norma Everson, *The Indian Metropolis: A View Toward the West*, Yale University Press (New Haven, CT), 1989, pp 104–11; and Suhash Chakravarty, 'Architecture and politics in the construction of New Delhi', *Architecture + Design*, Vol 2, No 2, Jan/Feb 1986, p 76.
2. 'In focus: Charles Correa', *Architecture + Design*, Vol 8, No 5, Sept/Oct 1991, p 18.
3. Satish Grover, 'Charles Correa: A view from Delhi', *Architecture + Design*, Vol 8, No 5, Sept/Oct 1991, p 17.
4. Charles Correa, *Charles Correa*, Thames & Hudson (London), 1996, p 220.
5. Kenneth Frampton, 'The work of Charles Correa', in ibid, p 14.
6. Kenneth Frampton, 'Towards a critical regionalism: Six points for an architecture of resistance', in Hal Foster (ed), *The Anti-Aesthetic: Essays on Postmodern Culture*, Bay Press (Port Townsend, WA), 1983, p 26.
7. Manu Desai and Jutta Jain are listed as 'mythology' consultants for Correa's Jawahar Kala Kendra in 'In focus: Charles Correa', op cit, p 24.

Text © 2007 John Wiley & Sons Ltd. Images: pp 56, 57(b), 58 © Reinhold Martin; p 57(t) © Mindspace; p 59 © Kazi Ashraf

# Material Formations

With much of the earlier assurances in tatters – whether the grandiose humanism of modernity or the ethnocentrism of a regional architecture – many architects are seeking a basis for their work in the fundamental ontology of material formation and site entrenchment. Siting and materiality were explored earlier in some of the work of Achyut Kanvinde, Balkrishna Doshi and Laurie Baker, but only to be superseded, first, by a turn towards scenography and mythography, and second by the more recent embrace of geography-free metal and glass panels (as a literal cover-up of the messy concrete hulks that most constructions in India are about). The fine art of building is retained in the projects featured in this section, as a demonstration of both the substantiality and sustainability of architecture in an age of reproduction and arbitrariness.

With glass as the holy grail of global architecture, and the emergence of ever-new materials and processes, concrete, stone and brick still maintain a material importance for the subcontinent, something that they owe undeniably to the work of Le Corbusier and Louis Kahn. The mutually expressive relationship of structure and tectonics is yet to be exhausted, especially if there is a compelling sociological argument behind it. Much of the Indian context still claims a sort of Gandhian ethos of economically minded indigenous construction that arises from the parameters of site and local culture. But, in fact, a big degree of building involves cladding that disrupts the primacy of territory and localness as well as tectonic uprightness, as explored by Reinhold Martin in his earlier essay in this issue.

Materiality and the process of making are gaining ground in both ethical and ecological terms, as explored in the work of Anupama Kundoo in this section. This is established in other projects ranging from the much admired work of Laurie Baker to the recent works of Anil Laul. Materiality and making also offer opportunities for architects, whether in a Neomodernist or a paratraditional vein, to create a phenomenal and sensual ensemble rich in visual and tactile terms. The work of Urbana, featured in this section, is an example of the former, while the work of Gerard da Cunha's Architecture Autonomous, also in this section, is evidence of the latter. Urbana's architects' residence in Dhaka displays their Modernist mastery of crafting in the long list of materials deployed: brick, teak, travertine, porcelain chips, glass, copper, steel, offset plates, gun metal and recycled materials (bricks recovered from a demolished building site). In addition, architects such as Samira Rathod (see the 'Mumbai Architects' section) and Aniket Bhagwat have explored the material dimension in the context of landscape design, producing enormously poetic constructions.

That building is also about being emplaced in a particular site and location, making materiality integral to landscape decisions, is demonstrated in the work of Vastu Shilpa Consultants' Rajeev Kathpalia, shown in this section, as well some of the projects by Studio Mumbai Architects and Rahul Mehrotra (see 'Mumbai Architects'). Kathpalia's work also engages larger narratives, either ecological or cosmological in nature. The meticulous and poetic crafting evident in most of these projects is instructive of an architectural passion that too often is a victim of either instant gratification or accelerated consumerism.

# Matharoo Associates (Gurjit Singh Matharoo)

The recent work of Ahmedabad-based Matharoo Associates reinvigorates the concrete language of Le Corbusier and Kahn, and the early works of Indian Modernists, but is rendered with a more slender and lighter disposition. Projects from private residences to public facilities brandish a rough, impenetrable shell that conceals a cocoon of animated space; a difference of materiality also amplifies the contrast. Gurjit Singh Matharoo brings to his practice his earlier experiences in Bhutan, Dubai and Locarno. He is also passionate about product design, especially automobiles, having designed mobile blood-donation vans and carried out research in advanced motorcycle design.

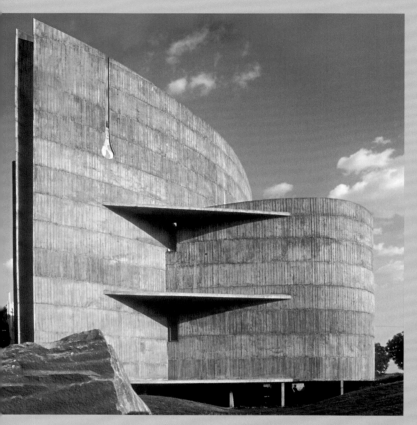

## Prathama Blood Center, Ahmedabad, 2000

The design for India's most modern and largest blood centre, the clients for which are pioneers in the field of blood transfusion and processing, required a new building type that is more of a playful programme than a service-intensive functional entity, and which removes the repulsion associated with medical facilities by transforming it into a receptive public domain. Working with limited space and a low budget, Matharoo thus opted for a solid, concrete exterior that houses an animated, light-filled and transparent interior.

## Cattiva mobile blood-donation van, 2005

As an extension to the Prathama Blood Centre, Matharoo designed a mobile blood-donation van in an effort to reach out to those parts of the population still reeling under the compulsions of family blood ties. The van has four automatic donor chairs, a medical examination cubicle, furnished pantry, chemical toilet and a refreshment area and lounge, and is constructed on a 1616 Tata chassis. With a capacity of 100 donations a day, it is projected that each Cattiva van, connected to blood banks throughout India, will bring about a silent revolution by making the stigma that currently surrounds donating blood a thing of the past.

## House for Ashok Patel, Ahmedabad, 2006

Located in a fast-growing suburb of Ahmedabad, the house was designed for a family consisting of a socially active couple, their teenage son and frequently visiting parents and relatives. It addresses the paradox of the increasingly reclusive modern suburban house by referring to the inward-looking traditional houses (the 'pols') of the area on the one hand, and the 'open plot dwelling' best exemplified by Le Corbusier's Shodan House, also in Ahmedabad, on the other.

A central void is framed by two blocks on the long side and compound walls on the shorter side. While the house turns its back on the street and the anonymous neighbourhood, it still manages to draw in the breeze, greenery, rain, sun and sky through varying degrees of openness. The columns, walls and beams appear to be woven into an intricate lattice which becomes animated when the strong sun falls on it. The epitome of the filigree is a 50-millimetre (2-inch) thick stair entirely cantilevered on its risers and composed as a square helix.

## Ashwinikumar Crematorium, Surat, Gujarat, 1999

The crematorium was the result of a national competition that was necessary after plague and communal riots left the city in a condition of filth and squalor. Located next to the Tapi River, the plan of the crematorium is the outcome of a detailed study of Hindu rituals and their architectural interpretation. Within its Brutalist concrete shell, the structure accommodates all the processional and ritual elements associated with the cremation service, including the sacred dip into the river. However, the vocabulary of the building is kept secular in nature, opening the place to all, irrespective of their religious beliefs.

Text ©© 2007 John Wiley & Sons Ltd. Images: p 62(tl) © Gurjit Singh, Matharoo Associates; pp 62(r&b) © Matharoo Associates; p 62(cl) © Chandan, S, Matharoo Associates; p 63(t) © Joginder Singh; p 63(b) Dinesh Mehta

# Anupama Kundoo

Informed by research into and experimentation with eco-friendly construction methods, the work of Anupama Kundoo adheres to the fundamentals of Indian tectonics in forming its architectural language. In this respect her work is influenced by the experimental environment of Auroville, and the construction innovations of Balkrishna Doshi and Laurie Baker. In 1990 she started her architecture practice in Auroville, a place she describes as an international city in the making in southeast India (see her essay in this issue). From 1992 to 1996 she lived in Berlin and worked in social housing, before returning to Auroville.

## Wall House, Auroville, 2000

Kundoo's own residence embodies her research and experimentation in three primary areas: eco-friendly building materials and technology as alternatives to current building trends, energy efficiency, and a climate-responsive building language. An eco-friendly infrastructure for the management of water, waste and energy was also part of her exploration here.

The house, oriented to the southeast for maximum air circulation, is basically a narrow 2.2-metre (7.2-foot) long vaulted space within brick masonry, with the various activities arranged in a row, as in a train. Each activity spills over on the northeast side in the form of alcoves and projections, and on the southwest under the large 4-metre (13-foot) overhang provided by the main vaulted roof.

The structure is organised by insulated roofs and modular materials: the exposed brick walls revive the use of traditional bricks (*achakal*) set in lime mortar with raked joints, and catenary vaults using hollow clay tubes have been used for climatic insulation as well as for reducing the unnecessary use of steel in '*pucca*' (permanent) roofs. Some of the flat roofs have been constructed using hollow burnt-clay trapezoidal extruded modules, specially manufactured locally as a solution for flat-roof insulation, over part-precast beams. In the intermediate floor, terracotta pots were used as fillers to increase the effective depth of concrete while minimising the volume of concrete and steel in the slabs.

The house is defined by clear lines and masses, yet the inside and outside spaces are blurred. The southwest facade is a transparent wooden structure with a mesh to allow a full view of the sunset, while the vault overhang provides adequate shade and ensures that the heat and the glare of the direct sun do not reach the cool interiors.

## Creativity, Auroville, 2003

Creativity is the first part of a larger housing development, Harmony, in one of Auroville's residential zones. The Creativity development will provide accommodation for approximately 360 residents along with common spaces on a 2.17-hectare (5.4-acre) site. The residents are grouped in smaller, independently managed communities of 50 to 60 people sharing common facilities. The project also aims to achieve cost-effective, attractive, functional housing of low environmental impact against the background of the acute shortage of housing in the area.

Auroville replicates the issues of many urban centres where people of diverse backgrounds come to live and work together. The Creativity housing project is intended to be a model of how Auroville's aims can be reflected in the details of home life.

## Pierre's House, Auroville, 1992

Pierre's House displays a climatic modulation, with vaulted roofs made of terracotta tubes, cavity walls at the exteriors, and ferrocement fins that regulate the glare and yet allow the free movement of prevailing winds.

Text © 2007 John Wiley & Sons Ltd. Images: pp 64, 65(b) © Andreas Deffner; p 65(t) © Aurovici Sarcomanens

# Vastu Shilpa Consultants (Rajeev Kathpalia)

As a partner in Vastu Shilpa Consultants in Ahmedabad, established by the master architect Balkrishna Doshi, Rajeev Kathpalia makes his own commentary on the cosmic and mythological dimension of architecture and thus continues the larger-than-building imperatives of the practice. Besides being an intersection of the seen and the unseen, and the current and archaic, his buildings and projects are deeply imbued with a landscape and territorial dimension of architecture.

## Arjun Machan, Ahmedabad, 2004

The structure here is almost non-existent – 'only a verandah', and hence a *machan* (platform) – but it implies the world near and far. Designed as a weekend retreat on an agricultural land outside Ahmedabad, the *machan* was conceived as a viewing machine that takes in the full panorama of the landscape: the rising of the sun and moon and the movement of the stars, as well as the diverse animal and botanical vignettes towards the distant horizon.

A verandah is traditionally attached to a house, but in this case there is no house. From inside, the *machan* is an informal, uninterrupted living space. On the outside it is a latticework of steel and glass attached to a brick wall. In addition, nothing in the *machan* is at right-angles and nothing is symmetrical. The structure extends itself into the landscape in myriad ways: thick brick walls stand without supporting anything, grassy mounds enclose a vegetable garden within shallow ridges and valleys, strategically located seats offer unexpected gatherings and views. There is also a series of lily ponds, an open-to-sky kitchen and dining area, and two tall brick piers holding a spout that pours water from up high into a long swimming pool.

On a clear winter's night when Orion charts his course through the heavens, this ensemble of natural brick walls, stand-alone brick columns and the curved form of the verandah seem, like the Jantar Mantar observatory, to track his movement.

## Imax Theatre, Ahmedabad, 2002

Part of the 100-hectare (247-acre) 'Science City', the Imax Theatre is a crucial node for both the emergent mediatisation of the country and the shadows of ancient mythologies. The core of the complex includes two theatres – a 651-seat 2-D theatre and a 556-seat 3-D theatre – as well as a speciality restaurant, a 3-D visual-reality video-game parlour and a cyber café. The visitor experience is intended to oscillate between the 'Natural and Manmade, Virtuality and Reality while moving through the site'. The technological nature of the theatre is dialogically counterbalanced by the mythopoeic elements of the civic plaza with its lotus and water symbolism.

The plaza provides a civic space for the citizens of Ahmedabad where one is sorely lacking, with its aquatic elements and a demonstration of the ecologically sustainable performance of the complex (including the production of vegetables by hydroponics for consumption in the cafeteria and restaurant). The plaza is also the fulcrum around which the sequence of entering and exiting the complex revolves, an itinerary that includes an exhibition on nature and technology and culminates in the theatre. Its subterranean disposition is also both technical and mythopoeic.

Text © 2007 John Wiley & Sons Ltd. Images © Rajeev Kathpalia, Vastu Shilpa Consultants, Ahmedabad, photos Rajeev Kathpalia

# Architecture Autonomous (Gerard da Cunha)

Gerard da Cunha maintains his practice from the old Portuguese colony of Goa, which he considers has a novel history in that it was the site of the 'first sustained encounter between the East and the West'. This encounter has engendered a unique culture and architecture that is evident in da Cunha's lively and rather Gaudíesque work.

## Nrityagram Dance Village, Bangalore, 1994

Established by dancer and teacher Protima Gauri as a model residential 'dance village', this was the first of its kind for Indian classical dancing. The architectural project derives its inspiration and construction methodology from the local vernacular of a region rich in materials and building practice. The methodology of design was an evolutionary one, with many on-site additions and modifications creating buildings of a lyrical nature often arranged to enclose space or as backdrops for dance.

'I dream of building a community of dancers in a forsaken place amidst nature,' says Gauri, 'a place where nothing exists except dance. A place where you breathe, eat, sleep, dream, talk, imagine – dance. A place where all the five senses can be refined to perfection ... A place called Nrityagram.'

## Museum of Traditional Goan Architecture, near Panjim, Goa, 2004

The building of a small museum as a 'traffic island' here became an occasion for affecting the larger setting by creating something that 'had to look "crazy" enough in the tradition of museum buildings (Bilbao and Guggenheim) which would seduce the local vegetable seller into buying a ticket.' Though situated 7 kilometres (4.3 miles) from the town of Panjim and 2 kilometres (1.2 miles) from a national highway, the setting of the acute-angled site is an enchanted valley and a genuine sacred grove. The architectural brief included creating a village core with urban design considerations, and controlling the traffic to a neighbouring playschool and organising the parking.

In the triangulated building there is a reception at one corner and a café at the other, with the two ends supported on giant grinding stones. Da Cunha turned the corners using a corbel (the most basic of traditional structural systems), and added a verandah to the south and part of the auditorium to the north, both of which are simply supported and resting on props.

According to da Cunha: 'Coming down the road on the east, the building looks like the *Titanic*, which is what the villagers call it. It could also pass for a fish waiting to swallow you up. From the south it looks like the set of a play ... I'm sometimes asked why the metaphor of a ship. Well the honest truth is that this was quite accidental, but when I noticed it, I played along and added the waves.'

Text © 2007 John Wiley & Sons Ltd. Images © Gerard da Cunha

# Urbana

Based in Dhaka, Bangladesh, and originally formed by Kashef Mahboob Chowdhury and Marina Tabassum, the work of Urbana displays a heightened sense of material crafting within an invigorated Modernist ethos that has earned awards for the practice and been featured in many international publications.

### A5 architects' residence, Dhaka, Bangladesh, 2002

For architects Kashef Mahboob Chowdhury and Marina Tabassum, planning the space on the sixth and topmost floor of an apartment building that they also designed offered an opportunity to create a 'pavilion in the air' in a 111-square-metre (1,200-square-foot) area. While conceived of as an interiorised refuge within Dhaka's notorious urbanity, the apartment opens out to the environment in poetically calculated ways to repossess the delights of rain, sun and the rarer tropical breeze.

The locus of the apartment is the 'room for rain', an open-air space where the gentle sound of fountain water (if it is not raining), the sweet smell of jasmine or the flickering of the niched candles at night imbue the architectural space with choreographed sound, smell and mood.

Throughout the apartment, a palette of colours and textures display the architects' Modernist mastery of materials and crafting. The list of materials is long: brick, teak, travertine, porcelain chips, glass, copper, steel, offset plates, gun metal, recycled materials (such as bricks recycled from a demolished building site), operable window panels (*kharkhari*), and an entire door of brick that swings out towards the bathroom.

### NEK10, Dhaka, 2001

A two-storeyed residence for two brothers, each occupying his own floor, this low-budget project simply resorted to addressing the challenge of having a busy street to the front and the need for a functional layout with enough light and ventilation.

Text © 2007 John Wiley & Sons Ltd. Images © Kashef/Urbana

# In Depth
## Inscribing the Indian Landscape

**When India was colonised by the British in the 18th and 19th centuries, it was systematically surveyed and delineated in map form for administrative and political purposes. Here, Anuradha Mathur and Dilip da Cunha urge a new, 'deeper' reading of the landscape that fully acknowledges the multiple uses and potential initiations of public spaces.**

Landscape in India has a powerful design agency that resides neither in the picturesque scene nor in the increasingly popular notion of a surface that takes its measure from infrastructural, economic and ecological processes and transactions that operate behind the scene. Rather it lies in an extraordinary depth of amorphous matter, a flux that can be configured and reconfigured in infinite ways. This depth has been probed time and again in the past in moments of enterprise and colonisation to draw out 'things' and articulate new terrains that serve as vocabularies and grounds for design practices. Yet this primordial act is largely unacknowledged by designers of the built environment in India today, allowing the terrain in place to go largely unquestioned and for India's rich depth to remain largely unengaged.

The terrain in place today was drawn out by British surveyors beginning in the 18th century in a land they saw as *terra incognita*, and described by them through maps, gazetteers and administrative and educational practices in terms of town and country, land and water, public and private, building and open space. Today this terrain can no longer be defended convincingly. The lines between these dichotomous entities have become increasingly blurred as much in everyday life as in catastrophe, threatening the many disciplines and practices that work to maintain their separations, but also exposing these entities as wishful individuations of an era disposed towards drawing clear and distinct boundaries. It is a cultivated literacy and, despite the thickness, even fluidity, given to boundaries today as thresholds, temporal margins and unique ecologies, it is difficult to shake off the surveyor's delineations; indeed the surveyor's imagination that is so embedded in the field and vocabulary of design.

There is an urgent need to draw out a new terrain. More importantly, perhaps, there is a need to recover depth as an active ingredient in design practice. This promises not merely a new terrain, but an agile one that can take on more effectively and creatively the increasing openness of today's economies and ecologies. One glimpses signs of this agility beyond the reach of administration and education, in the

street, the bazaar, but perhaps most evidently in the maidan. This enigmatic landscape, prevalent across India yet lost in translation, offers a way to imagine and operationalise depth in design practices that aspire to a much needed agility and tenacity in the Indian landscape.

### Maidan

As a word, 'maidan' has resisted translation from its Persian origin, inserting itself in English conversations in India and elsewhere. As a landscape, however, it is consumed by more than one translation. *Hobson-Jobson* describes it as 'an open space, an esplanade, parade-ground or green, in or adjoining a town; a *piazza* (in the Italian sense); any open plain with grass on it; a *chaugan* ground; a battle-field.'[1] This is a wide array of descriptions by association with spatial entities that the eye can see and the cartographer can plot. Indeed the word 'maidan' today is commonly used to refer to demarcated open spaces in settlements across the Indian subcontinent such as the Oval and Azad maidans in Mumbai. 'The character of these spaces is modest and devoid of embellishment. Their simple emptiness stands in stark contrast to the intricate urban fabric surrounding them. Rarely thought of or described as designed landscapes, these places do not call attention to themselves, yet they continue to support a wide spectrum of urban life from cricket, football and other sports to trade fairs and circuses, from political rallies and religious congregations to the grazing of goats.'[2]

This imaging of the maidan, however, as a demarcated commons inscribed by a multiplicity of uses is a particular translation of the maidan: a place released from the confines of programme, but held by space. As such it belongs less with the nomadic sensibility of the Persian heritage of the word and more with an ambitious European project: the portrayal of the Indian subcontinent as a spatially articulate terrain. This project, which operated primarily through the map, goes back to Ptolemy's 2nd-century representation, *India intra Gangem* ('India up to the Ganges', or 'India proper'). In the 18th century it was seriously undertaken by route surveyors of the East India Company, and in the 19th century it reached a new level of mathematical precision in the Great Trigonometrical Survey of India (GTS), which simultaneously measured the curvature of the earth and positioned objects on its surface. This project, which exhausted the surface of the subcontinent through the delineations of the map, paralleled the emergence of the map as a powerful tool not just for representing land, but for administering it as well.

The maidan was not exempt from this project. Perceived as part of a spatially articulate surface it was drawn by surveyors as an entity along with states, districts, towns, forts, buildings, fields, gardens, roads and water bodies. Indeed the promise of the GTS was the representation of all the 'objects' that comprise the land as they truly were 'upon the globe'.

What surveyors take for granted is the bounded nature of 'things' in order to facilitate their presentation in maps. They see boundaries and edges not only where they are not obvious, as in dynamic and fluid places like deltas, coasts or even settlements, but also where they are not necessary constituents of cultural imagination. It is a seeing that cannot be taken for granted. Suspending the eye of the surveyor, then, promises another translation of the maidan, one that is released from both programme *and* space.

Gandhi, that great resistor of the map, ventured this translation each time he gathered on the Sabarmati, a name that some know as a maidan while others educated in the vocabulary of the surveyor know as a river or, for much of the year before it was made perennial by those seeking a 'riverfront' for the 'city' of Ahmedabad, a river bed. His assemblies on the Sabarmati, out of convenience perhaps, but also to evade authorities who discouraged him from using public spaces in the city, suggest that the maidan is not there to be described as much as there when initiated. At this point the Sabarmati is not confined to a river bed, but is acknowledged as a name that has just accommodated another unique terrain, one that gathers its own duration and commands its own extension. Besides Gandhi (and the monsoons), the Sabarmati accommodates other initiators of terrains, each with its own duration and extension: pedestrians, players, the *gujri* (flea market) and market, goats, grasses, dyers, alluvia and so on. This Sabarmati is not limited by either the surveyor's typology of a river, or by the extent of a river bed; instead it gathers and extends by multiple terrains and potential initiations.

This translation of the maidan as a name with a propensity for durations and extensions belongs in a landscape where names do not signify objects in a land exhausted by categories of use and spatial demarcations as much as a multiplicity of terrains and possible initiations. It makes for an Indian landscape that is not the subject of maps, but one where the GTS represents just one initiation among many.

We explore this Indian landscape through an investigation of Bangalore where the terrain of the GTS began. We suggest that design practice on the maidan does not work with a described landscape as much as it inscribes new terrains that gather and extend by measures of their own making.[3]

## Inscribing the Bangalore Maidan

The terrain of the GTS draws attention to one name: Bangalore, or *Bengaluru*. In popular imagination this name refers to a city, an entity bound as much by its title Garden City (garden implying enclosure) as it is by statistics, narratives, and the planners' desire to enclose it with a green belt. However, to William Lambton, a major in the English army that defeated Tipu Sultan in 1799, it was first an open terrain that offered an excellent opportunity to begin from a 'centrical situation' on the peninsula 'an uninterrupted series of triangles [from the Malabar coast to the Coromandel coast], and of continuing that series to an almost unlimited extent in every direction.'[4] His enterprise, which became known as the GTS, revealed the openness of Bangalore, but it also set in motion practices and disciplines that would limit Bangalore, as it would a host of names, including India, to a spatial entity in design and popular imagination.

Just beneath the surface initiated by Lambton, however, is a Bangalore that would continue to anchor terrains that resist the surveyor's surface. This Bangalore is not held to the surveyor's typology of a city, municipal limits or a metropolitan region. It is, like the Sabarmati, a name with a propensity for terrains of many durations and extensions; in short, it is a maidan.

Detail of Jean Nicolas Bellin's *Carte reduite de la Presque Isle de l'Inde*, c 1750. Like most places on the Indian subcontinent in the mid-18th century, Bangalore, or *Bengaluru*, was a name on maps that held out the prospect of multiple initiations.

Detail of the index chart to the Great Trigonometrical Survey of India, initiated in Bangalore in 1800.

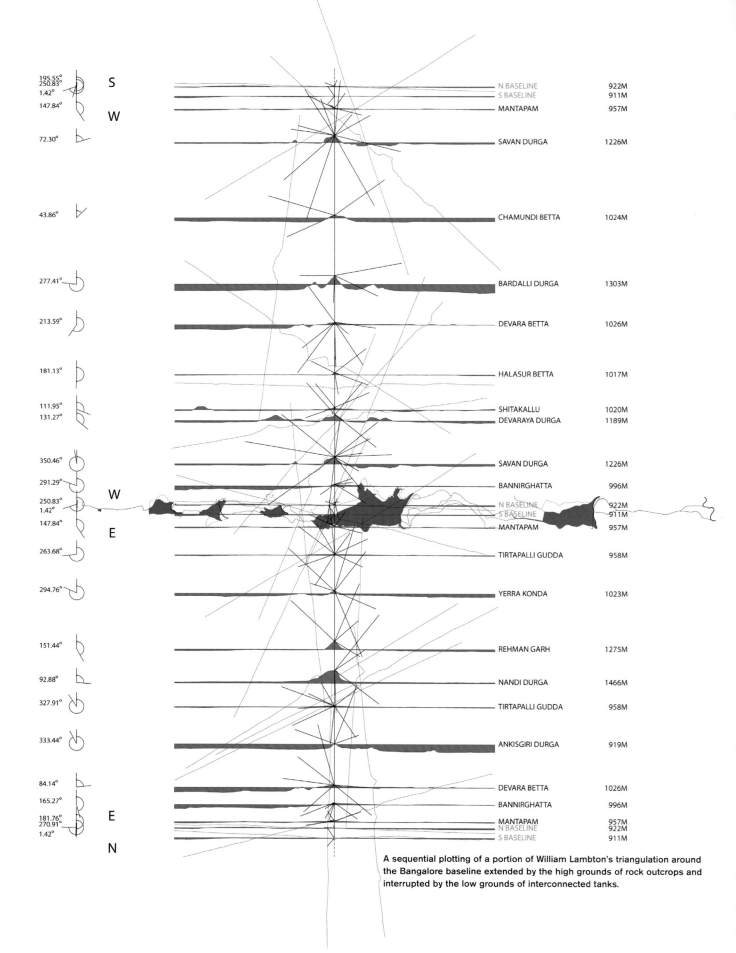

S

195.55°
250.83°
1.42°

147.84°

W

72.30°

43.86°

277.41°

213.59°

181.13°

111.95°
131.27°

350.46°

291.29°

250.83°
1.42°

W

147.84°

E

263.68°

294.76°

151.44°

92.88°

327.91°

333.44°

84.14°

165.27°

181.76°
270.91°
1.42°

E

N

N BASELINE          922M
S BASELINE          911M
MANTAPAM            957M

SAVAN DURGA         1226M

CHAMUNDI BETTA      1024M

BARDALLI DURGA      1303M

DEVARA BETTA        1026M

HALASUR BETTA       1017M

SHITAKALLU          1020M
DEVARAYA DURGA      1189M

SAVAN DURGA         1226M

BANNIRGHATTA        996M

N BASELINE          922M
S BASELINE          911M

MANTAPAM            957M

TIRTAPALLI GUDDA    958M

YERRA KONDA         1023M

REHMAN GARH         1275M

NANDI DURGA         1466M

TIRTAPALLI GUDDA    958M

ANKISGIRI DURGA     919M

DEVARA BETTA        1026M

BANNIRGHATTA        996M

MANTAPAM            957M
N BASELINE          922M
S BASELINE          911M

A sequential plotting of a portion of William Lambton's triangulation around the Bangalore baseline extended by the high grounds of rock outcrops and interrupted by the low grounds of interconnected tanks.

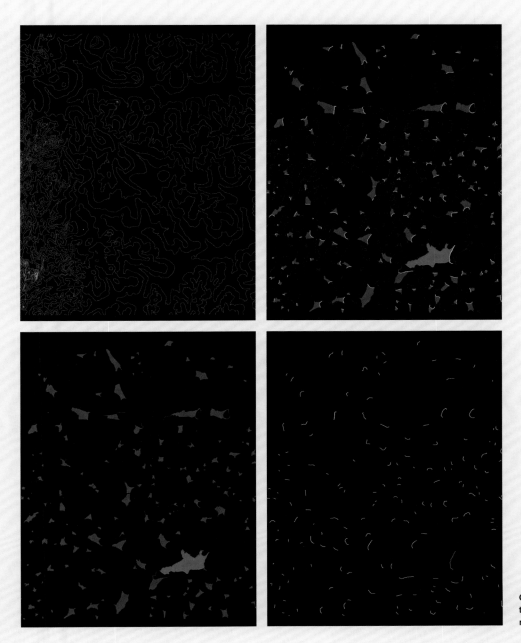

Clockwise from top left: Bangalore topography; Bangalore tanks; Bangalore networks; Bangalore bunds.

## Terrain 1: Bangalore Baseline

The GTS began with the measurement of a baseline. Thereafter surveyors moved from point to point or rather highpoint to highpoint, computing distances with the help of angles of triangles. They were facilitated in this by massive granite outcrops, most of them isolated and some reaching up to 400 metres (1,312 feet) above the gently undulating land. These outcrops provided the extended views necessary to connect the apexes of triangles with the help of a theodolite. Each triangle carried forward the length of the baseline through computation. Each also anchored smaller triangles in a web of points that gripped the land in fine detail, holding it firm on paper so that movements, changes and, importantly, territorial violations on the ground could be registered.

The most movement was in the lowlands. These lands were crossed by embankments that impounded water in what the English called 'tanks'. One of these tanks, Belandur Tank, was particularly disruptive. Two-thirds of the way and six weeks into the measurement of the baseline it extended across the line, forcing its re-measurement. In time, however, surveyors would hold this tank and the many others on this terrain firm, at least on paper.

Maps of this surface inscribed over the last two centuries by roads, rails, property lines, pipelines, open spaces and other infrastructures continue to inform the popular imagination as they do city plans and design. Tanks on this terrain, delineated with a line and coloured blue in maps, have easily morphed into scenic lakes or been drained off to become 'land' for housing, stadiums and bus depots.

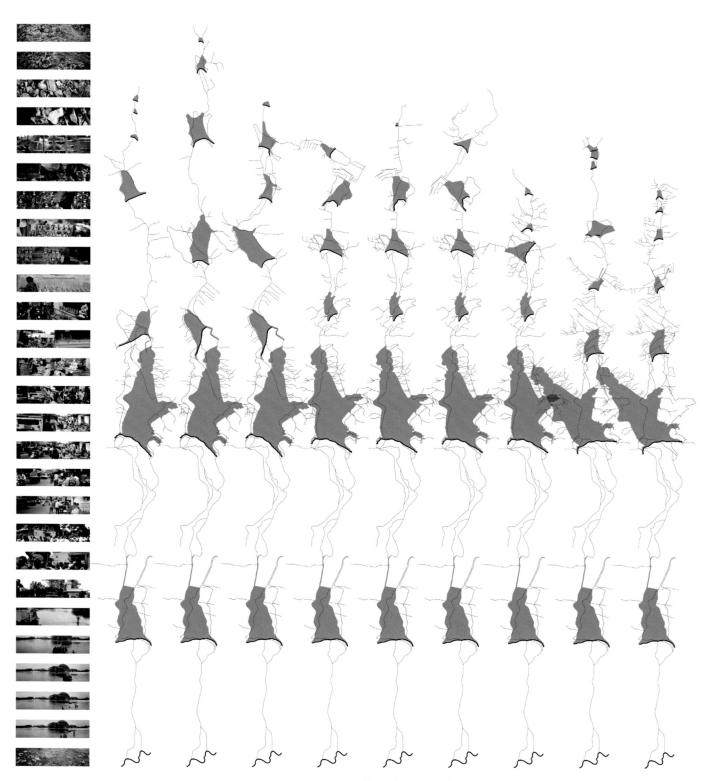

The series and parallels of Bangalore's *keres* operate between two ends of a clay economy: a dry bed that provides the material for Ganapathi idols, and the full tank that allows for the immersion of these idols following the rains.

Photowork of the Belandur *kere*
bund (embankment).

## Terrain 2: Bangalore *Kere*

Often translated from its Kannada roots as tank, *kere* resists the isolation that has allowed tanks to be made into scenic lakes. It refers instead to a terrain initiated in the construction of a bund – an earthen embankment – and extended by run-offs. These run-offs of water, but also silt and clay eroded off the gneissic terrain, are organised not so much by flows as they are by overflows via sluices and weirs engineered into each bund. There are many possible lines to this overflow; they are all worked by political alliances as much as by physical relations of slope and topography.

When waters recede in the *kere* following the end of the rains, plants are accommodated and clay and silt are harvested. It is a movement from wetness to dryness that, with some imagination, can still be registered today in the Ganapathi festival, where the deity made from clay harvested from the *kere* moves through markets, temples and homes till it is finally immersed in the *kere* after the rains.

There are times when the *kere* is available for other activities – fairs, camps, festivities and sports. Indeed for much of the year, and sometimes for more than a year, the *kere* does not appear anything like the water bodies or lakes that people often expect to see in the 'tank' today.

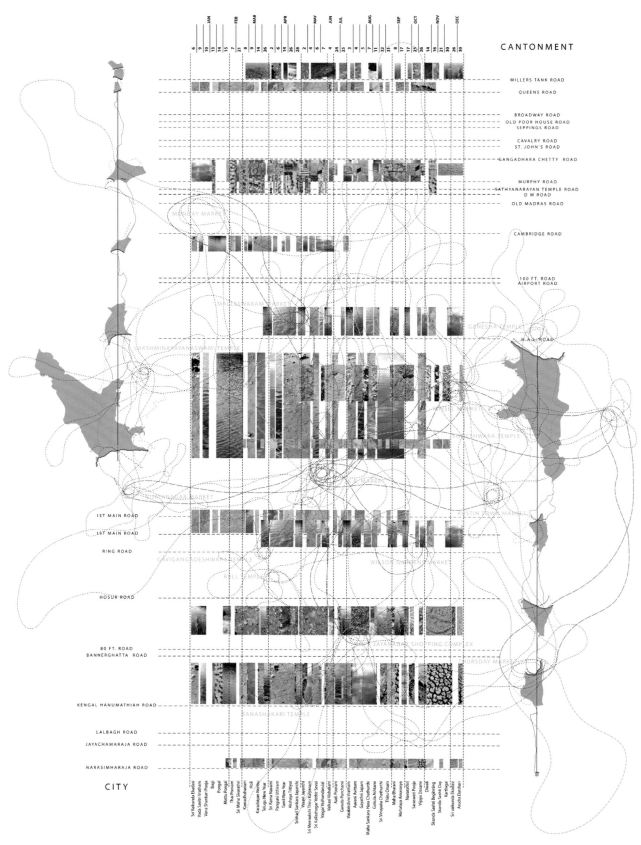

CANTONMENT

MILLERS TANK ROAD
QUEENS ROAD

BROADWAY ROAD
OLD POOR HOUSE ROAD
SEPPINGS ROAD
CAVALRY ROAD
ST. JOHN'S ROAD
GANGADHARA CHETTY ROAD
MURPHY ROAD
SATHYANARAYAN TEMPLE ROAD
D M ROAD
OLD MADRAS ROAD

CAMBRIDGE ROAD

100 FT. ROAD
AIRPORT ROAD

H. A. L. ROAD

1ST MAIN ROAD
1ST MAIN ROAD
RING ROAD

HOSUR ROAD

80 FT. ROAD
BANNERGHATTA ROAD

KENGAL HANUMATHIAH ROAD

LALBAGH ROAD
JAYACHAMARAJA ROAD

NARASIMHARAJA ROAD

CITY

A proposal for the temporal and material rhythms of the *tota* as it appropriates Bangalore's *keres*.

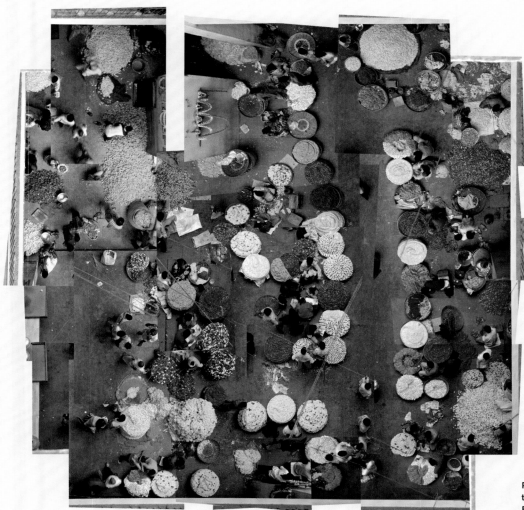

Photowork of the flower courtyard of the Krishna Rajendra (KR) Market, Bangalore.

## Terrain 3: Bangalore *Tota*

Bangalore's reputation as a Garden City developed largely as a result of its many parks, lakes, trees, tree-lined avenues and gardens, but also because of a botanical and horticultural enterprise at its centre: Lalbagh. Once the possession of Tipu Sultan, these gardens were taken over by the British in 1800 to cultivate plants for troops, and also to anchor and generate flows of useful and exotic plants across the world. They continue to operate on an open terrain inscribed by global trajectories of plant movements and local trajectories of cultivation, not merely in the vicinity of Bangalore City and Cantonment but across the Indian subcontinent.

This terrain is less an enclosure that thrives on difference from its surroundings as implied by the etymology of the word garden, and is more a *tota*. Although often translated as garden from its Kannada heritage, *tota* is an open, dynamic and working terrain for cultivation, but also a web of activity including nurseries, markets and, importantly, *keres* (when waters recede).

The City Market, also known as the Krishna Rajendra (KR) Market, is on this terrain. Here the *tota* is used, among other things, for the threading and sale of flowers by string or weight; it extends from here to other markets, but also to homes, temples and ceremonies. Many of these flowers remain in movement in women's hair and on deities in vehicles. This terrain is only momentarily contiguous, operating by diverse and emergent calendars of festivals, by walks in a market that are dictated by the daily settlement of vendors, by acts of bargaining, and by the contingencies of a largely unpredictable infrastructure. ⚙

### Notes
1. Henry Yule and AC Burnell, *Hobson-Jobson: a glossary of colloquial Anglo-Indian words and phrases, and of kindred terms, etymological, historical, geographical and discursive*, J Murray (London), 1903.
2. Anuradha Mathur, 'Neither Wilderness nor Home: The Indian *Maidan*', in James Corner (ed), *Recovering Landscape: Essays in Contemporary Landscape Architecture*, Princeton Architectural Press (New York), 2000, pp 205–19.
3. This essay builds on the material of Anuradha Mathur's and Dilip da Cunha's *Deccan Traverses: The Making of Bangalore's Terrain*, Rupa & Co (Delhi), 2006.
4. William Lambton, 'An account of a method for extending a geographical survey across the peninsula of India', *Asiatic Researches*, Vol 7, 1803, p 312.

Text © 2007 John Wiley & Sons Ltd. Images © Anuradha Mathur and Dilip da Cunha

# The 'Background' in Bangalore

## Architecture and Critical Resistance in a New Modernity

As the centre of India's new information and biotechnology industries, Bangalore has been at the forefront of the country's globalisation. As **Prem Chandavarkar** explains, the city's architectural culture continues at the leading edge to be one of 'intellectualism', valuing 'the background', a sense of place and contextualism over the more brash facadism of other cities.

For the first four decades, independent India had a problematic relationship with her sense of history, perceiving the previous two centuries as belonging to an unfortunate colonisation that could not be considered a part of authentic history. This postcolonial discontinuity led to a development discourse that remained suspended between a sense of a glorious past and an anticipated technological modernity.

Initially this suspension caused architectural thought to swing across these two extremes. The 1950s saw a burst of historical revivalism, but by the 1960s revivalism had run its course, and with Chandigarh's influence a Corbusian idiom was soon established in the imagination and architectural language of architects as a symbol of the modernity that India anticipated. This established an umbilical cord of Western influence that continued even once the idiom of the Modern

Movement had run its course. When Postmodernism began to gain ground internationally in the 1980s, the quest for modernity became overlaid with an anxiety for cultural relevance, leading to architects validating work by citing precedents such as Fatehpur Sikri, Jaisalmer or Jaipur.

Although this trend was widely perceived as 'Indian architecture', in reality it was much more localised, and was largely produced by practices located in three cities towards the north and west: Delhi, Ahmedabad and Mumbai.[1] In Bangalore, and other cities in the south, the situation was quite different. The centre of gravity of the struggle for Indian independence lay along the Delhi-Ahmedabad-Mumbai axis, and the relative displacement of the south from this maelstrom, together with the south Indian's natural introspective algorithmic bent of mind, led to a radically different orientation. The major figures in the first generation of architects here (CR Narayana Rao, LN Chitale and Bennett Pithavadian in Chennai; Narayan Chandavarkar and Pesi Thacker in Bangalore; and Laurie Baker in Thiruvanthapuram) did not attempt to root their work in any conceptual construct of nationalist modernity, and favoured a perspective of contextual resolutions rather than overarching frameworks. There is little historical documentation on these pioneers, but from anecdotal evidence it appears that their preoccupation was more with quietly earning the respect of the local community than publicly foregrounding emblems of Indian modernity. They were uncomfortable with publicity. This was an architecture of the background.

With its predilection towards the recognition of individual didactic genius, the discipline of architecture has not given much consideration to a tradition of the background. Foregrounded positions produced for public consumption often deflect attention towards issues that are abstracted and fashionable, rather than towards inclusive relationships of ongoing value. The contextual orientation of the background encourages human empathy and respect for the inhabitant and other stakeholders in the architectural enterprise. And the project-specific orientation of design effort focuses towards the creation of a grounded 'sense of place', eschewing abstract symbolism.

But more importantly, an architecture of the background is predicated upon a very different notion of culture. To foreground a position, culture has first to be identified as a conceptual construct, whereas in a tradition of the background, culture is assumed to occur as a by-product of contextualised negotiation. So if the goal is to produce 'Indian-ness', it is not necessary to start with a symbolic language of national identity; one should just recognise that

The historical context
*Left:* **Revivalism – Hanumantha Rao Naidu, Vidhana Soudha (State Assembly), Bangalore, 1956.**
*Centre:* **The Corbusian idiom – Charles Correa, Visvesvaraya Centre, Bangalore, 1974.**
*Right:* **Instant globalism – Thomas Associates, Safina Towers, Bangalore, 2006.**

The architect as provocateur
*Top:* **Vivek Associates, St Mark's Complex, Bangalore, 2006.**
*Bottom:* **InFORM Architects, Tillany Museum, Hosur, Tamil Nadu, 1998.**

their legacy from having its deserved impact. The focus towards client empathy, when coupled with a lack of critical detachment, meant that powerful external pressures could easily derail established directions. As a result, these architects did not create the conceptual tools for stability, and their trajectory was shaken by the drastic spurt in south Indian urban growth rates in the 1980s. The exception was Laurie Baker in Kerala, who remained stable in a critical detachment provided by an explicitly articulated philosophy rooted in a combination of Gandhian influence and his Quaker roots.[3] Baker's alignment with the background can be seen from his discomfort with publicity, and his insistence that design could occur only through coming to terms with client, site and local tradition, but in his commitment to a philosophy an alternative role for theory is constructed. Theory is not seen as a foundational philosophy that guides practice; it is seen as providing an ethical anchor to the ongoing negotiations of culture, a means of critiquing practice in order to achieve a balanced connection to context.

This attitude was not found in Bangalore, and the tradition of the background began to waver. In the early 1990s the city began to experience metamorphic change. National policy reversed direction, and a regulated economy with an inward focus gave way to a liberalised regime aimed at global integration. This reformist wave was led by the new industries of information technology and biotechnology, and very soon these Indian industries became significant global players. Bangalore was a primary centre from which this change emerged. It came to be perceived as a vanguard city that would lead India's march into modernity in the 21st century, and moved from the background firmly into the foreground. In addition, the national development discourse that had been ingrained since independence disappeared. Modernity no longer had to be anticipated: with the Indian city anchored publicly in global production, modernity had arrived.

Globalisation allowed emerging segments of the Indian economy to secede from the local economy and orient towards the global. The architecture of these institutions sought to anchor in the space of flows rather than the space of places.[4] An information technology company may be more concerned with how its campus is perceived in California than the view from across the street. The new desires of this space of flows sought to overcome earlier constraints in construction technology. With the liberalisation of import tariffs, messy non-standardised site-based technologies could now be concealed behind the newly available materials of structural glazing and aluminium-composite panel cladding. This was seen as a quick solution for producing the imagery of global desires, and was quickly established as an architectural modernity of instant globalism.

In this era of predicaments, Bangalore's legacy of the background acquired a new lease of life with the emergence of a new generation of younger architects. The practices researched for this article as representative of the trend are Architecture Paradigm, CnT Architects, Hundredhands, Total

one is dealing with Indian sites, climate, people, and so on, and if one deals with each of these with rigour, then an Indian product is bound to occur. For a practitioner concern should focus on the structure and rigour of ongoing negotiations, rather than on a theory of culture. This is a fairly dramatic reorientation of the discipline, for the central question of 'What is architecture?' is now contextualised within a wider question of 'What is architectural practice?' Modernity is constructed from the ground up, rather than imported from predefined conditions.

In Bangalore, architectural practice established itself within a tradition of the background.[2] However, this first generation also contained an Achilles heel that prevented

Environment Systems, Mathew & Ghosh Architects, Mindspace, Vivek Associates and InFORM Architects, with the latter two detaching to explore the direction of 'the architect as provocateur'. This list would not constitute a full description of the current generation of the background, and an attempt at a complete list would probably contain close to 20 names. If one examines their histories it is difficult to find any common thread binding these architects – many of them have migrated from other parts of the country, and there are no common influences in terms of education or epochal events. Rather, it is the nature of Bangalore's history that attracted a particular kind of architect. First, the city's growth rate offered significant opportunities for work; second, a great deal of the growth came from new-technology companies who did not feel the constraints of convention; and third (and most important), the legacy of the background meant there were no predetermined labels against which one was forced to take a position. These conditions drew architects who sought to explore new possibilities in modernity free from the baggage of prevailing 'isms'; who valorised experiential richness over symbolic expression and a sense of place over intellectual meta-statement.

Like their predecessors, these practitioners do not seek to produce manifestos that put forward broad overarching positions, but what sets them apart is their intellectualism. It is clear from their work, and from conversations with them, that they believe every decision has to be well considered and researched so that the work exhibits the high degree of critical rigour that has gone into its production. While they do not by any means constitute a majority in the city, they are forming the leading edge – and if one goes by the amount of space given recently to covering their work in Indian journals, or national design awards won in the last three years, it appears that the perceived cutting edge of Indian architectural design is beginning to shift away from the earlier axis of Delhi-Ahmedabad-Mumbai towards Bangalore.

A few of them aligned with what had become a global trend in architecture, where architecture no longer sought to put forward coherent social meaning, but celebrated vitality and the disruption of conventional hierarchies: 'architecture's role is not to express an extant social structure, but to function as a tool for questioning that structure and revising it.'[5] A new avant-garde role was seen for the architect – the architect as artistic provocateur.

However, in this globalised world, overloaded with hyper-mobile information flow, is there space for the avant-garde? The information age has created an economy where the scarcest commodity is attention; for that is what information consumes.[6] A major means of grabbing attention is through novelty – and the avant-garde tend to be mined as producers

The quest to craft a building well
**Shibanee & Kamal Architects, The Good Earth apartment building for Total Environment Systems, Bangalore, 2002.**

Capturing 'event space'
*Left:* **Sanjay Mohe (Mindspace), NSR-GIV Centre, Indian Institute of Management, Bangalore, 2003.**
*Right:* **Sanjay Mohe (Mindspace), HLL Research Centre, Bangalore, 2006.**

of novelty. Their work is detached from its foundation in critical thinking, taken for its pure visuality, attached to the artist's status as an iconic individual and utilised as a means of capturing attention. So one gets the example of architects such as Frank Gehry or Zaha Hadid, who early in their careers positioned themselves as iconoclastic rebels, though one now finds them used as vehicles for mainstream branding.

Most of the new generation of Bangalore's architects remain detached from global trends and retain the highly contextualised orientation of their legacy. They intensely reject an instant globalism of slick facades, for it amounts to denigrating Bangalore as nothing more than a shallow clone of Singapore or Dubai. Their decision to align with the background is much more conscious than that of their predecessors. Bangalore is now a foreground city, and this choice of the background is seen as crucial to constructing critical resistance to a superficial globalism that is more insidious than the earlier drive towards nationalism. They draw from local and global references, but distil this

absorption through the discriminating lens of a contemporary aesthetic in order to construct a palpable sense of place. However, they do not seek to theorise on any stable definition of place, and would probably agree that place, like practice, must be continuously negotiated.[7] They are much more comfortable talking in terms of individual projects rather than any overall thread in their work, and their sense of rigour is oriented towards process rather than product.

The choice of remaining in the background has now become problematic. Besides the foregrounding of Bangalore, the work of these architects is attracting public recognition, creating cause to wonder whether the introspective intellectualism that forms the foundation of this tradition could become compromised. However, are the extremes of foreground and background the only possible positions? Could there be a middle ground that retains the quiet introspective core, yet subjects that core to a critique of negotiation? If these architects have emulated Laurie Baker to stabilise their work within a sense of critical rigour, perhaps the time has

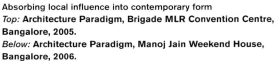

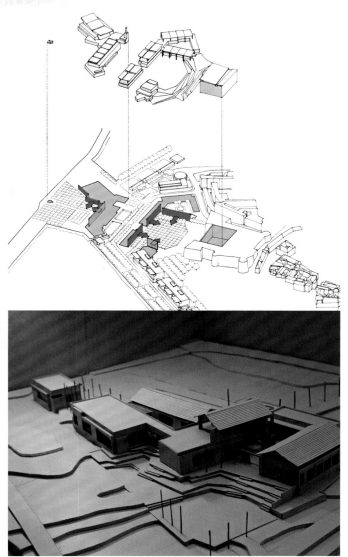

Absorbing local influence into contemporary form
*Top:* **Architecture Paradigm, Brigade MLR Convention Centre, Bangalore, 2005.**
*Below:* **Architecture Paradigm, Manoj Jain Weekend House, Bangalore, 2006.**

Seeking contextually appropriate form
*Top:* **Hundredhands, Proposal for the Waterfront, Crotone, Italy (competition entry for the 2006 Venice Biennale).**
*Bottom:* **Hundredhands, Hope Foundation Matriculation School, Puddupattinam, Tamil Nadu, 2007.**

come when it is necessary to raise the level of critique. This is a gap that urgently needs to be filled as there is no tradition of wider critique and review of work in order to seek out its underlying propositions. The practices in Bangalore remain relatively isolated, and are susceptible to a tendency in Indian architecture to rely on rhetoric rather than theory. The ethical dimension of Baker's philosophy is not given the attention it deserves. If the legacy of the background is to seek its full potential, it must realise that critical resistance can be sustained only when it is located within a critical culture. ⧄

**Notes**
1. As an example of this perception, see Vikram Bhatt and Peter Scriver, *After The Masters: Contemporary Indian Architecture*, Mapin Publishing (Ahmedabad), 1990. Of the 52 projects covered in this book, 41 are produced by architects located in one of these three cities.
2. The extent to which the tradition of the background took hold can be judged from the fact that Narayan Chandavarkar, who established the city's first architectural firm in 1947, spent two years in Chandigarh in the early 1960s yet remained detached from the dominant Corbusian current.
3. Laurie Baker, 'Of Architectural Truths and Lies', *The Hindu, Folio* Sunday magazine, 1 August 1999. Also available at http://www.hinduonnet.com/folio/fo9908/99080300.htm.
4. Manuel Castells, *The Rise of the Network Society*, Blackwell Publishing (Oxford), 2000.
5. Wikipedia entry on Bernard Tschumi: http://en.wikipedia.org/wiki/Bernard_Tschumi.
6. Michael H Goldhaber, 'The Attention Economy Hypothesis in Brief', http://goldhaber.org/blog/2006/08/30/the-attention-economy-hypothesis-in-brief/. Also see Herbert Simon, 'Designing organizations for an information-rich world', in Martin Greenberger (ed), *Computers, Communication and the Public Interest*, The Johns Hopkins Press (Baltimore, MD), 1971, pp 40–1.
7. See Doreen Massey, *For Space*, Sage Publications (London), 2005.

Text © 2007 John Wiley & Sons Ltd. Images: pp 78-9 © Prem Chandavarkar; p 80(t) © Vivek V Shankar; p 80(b) © InFORM Architects, photo S Viswanath; p 81 © Shibanee & Kamal Architects, photo Tarunn; p 82 © Courtesy Mindspace; p 83(tl&bl) © Architecture Paradigm Pvt Ltd; p 83(tr&br) © Bijoy Ramachandran/Hundredhands, drawing by Bijoy Ramachandran

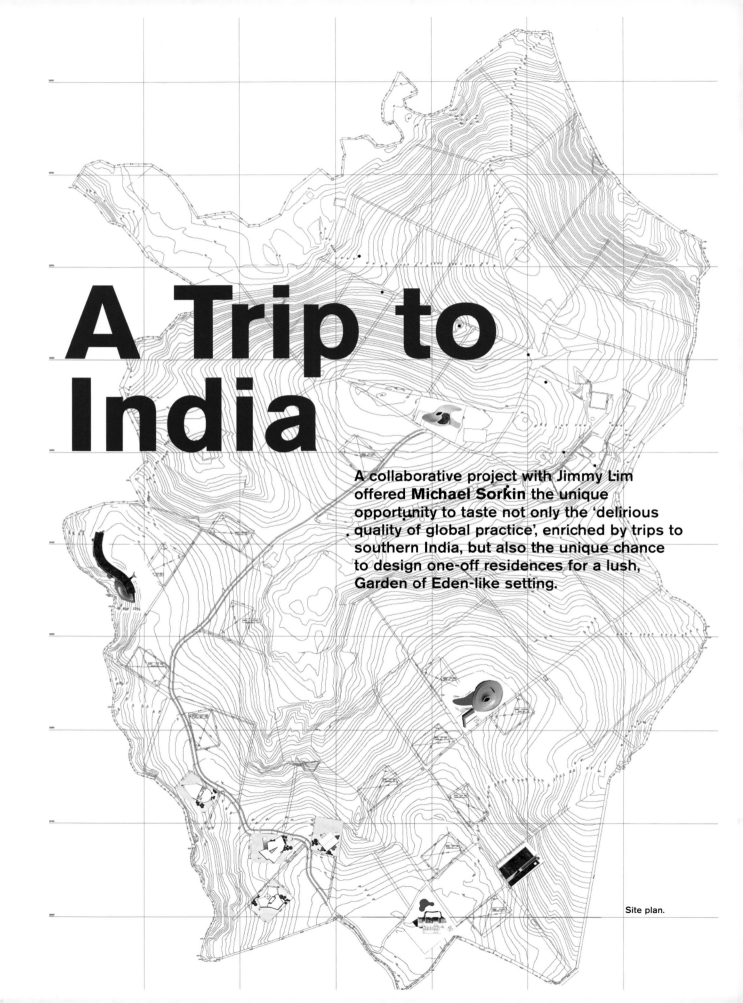

# A Trip to India

A collaborative project with Jimmy Lim
offered **Michael Sorkin** the unique
opportunity to taste not only the 'delirious
quality of global practice', enriched by trips to
southern India, but also the unique chance
to design one-off residences for a lush,
Garden of Eden-like setting.

Site plan.

**Project from Site 8.**

Invited by the Bangalore firm SMLXL to collaborate on a project for a group of houses in Coorg – a town near Mangalore in Karnataka – long-time friends Jimmy Lim and Michael Sorkin decided to set up a collaborative practice: Lim Sorkin Design (LSD). The name is meant not simply to be cheeky, but to suggest the inevitably delirious quality of global practice. Excited immersions in otherness are par for the contemporary course: trips. As architectural production is increasingly internationalised, its sites must be invented in mind, culture transduced, filtered imaginatively. Of course, every project demands familiar styles of due diligence, channelling of topography, climate, habit and desire. But there are no inevitable outcomes any more, even if sought. Where is the south Indian tradition of three-bedroom, time-share second homes in the hills for IT executives and their families, designed by architects from around the world?

The site in Coorg, filled with gifts, is demandingly beautiful. A working coffee plantation set in lush hills is as Edenic as it gets, supporting symbiotic cardamom and pepper cultivation as well as abundant wildlife. It will continue to produce these products at current levels and the 20-odd new houses – to be designed by a number of Indian and foreign architects – are obliged to fit in respectfully. Locations have been chosen by the plantation owner, a trained agronomist who has spent years walking the land and who knows it with remarkable intimacy. Best practices have been set out for the minimal use of energy, natural ventilation, on-site waste treatment and local materials. Carbon footprints will be neutral.

How then to proceed? Lim (LSD/KL) and Sorkin (LSD/NY) have taken slightly different approaches. Although both have imagined their groups of structures as families, the genetics vary. The four houses from LSD/KL, clustered on adjacent sites, have more intimate tectonic relations and detailing, and are intended to be seen as an ensemble, a little settlement in the forest. The five from LSD/NY are distributed on more distant and disconnected sites and are much more morphologically varied, while sharing a palette of details, especially for elements that are likely to be fabricated off site. Both groups are similar in area and programme, and both are intimately attuned to the particularities of sun, breeze, monsoon and view.

If there is a quality about these houses that might be described as 'Indian', it lies not simply in their environmental behaviour, but in a certain licence for latitude. Both Lim and Sorkin are frequent visitors to India and both have a history of intoxication with the place. Because of the country's astonishing diversity and because of the remarkable hybridities everywhere produced by the reciprocal inseminations of form, place and culture, Indian architecture can never be singular: the very thought is ludicrous and disrespectful. Saturated with difference, this is a place to drive thought and imagination, not to constrict it.

For Lim and Sorkin, this idea of the filtration of difference likewise liberated their joint practice from the low-odds task of trying to find some singular style on which to cooperate. Instead, both took their own histories and fertilised them with what attracted their eyes and hearts in this mad and magical place. Lim was perhaps more drawn to the simple trabeation and intricate detail of various wooden architectures, Sorkin to the convulsive form and coloration of Dravidian holy places. Were these influences direct? By no means. Are they legible? Perhaps not. Are they present? Without a doubt. ∆

**Site 1 (LSD/KL)**
Three individual spaces radiate from a central void with stairs that spiral around this opening. Walls are undefined with a shading device that spans three floors and allows constant ventilation.

**Site 2 (LSD/KL)**
Straddling a hillock, this structure is planned as two fingers that cantilever and protrude out over the valley with decks that overlook the voids in between.

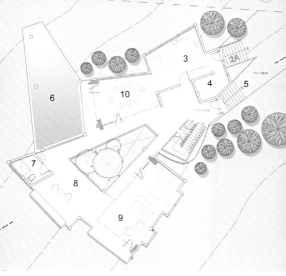

### Site 3 (LSD/KL)
Sitting on a steep site the entire western facade of this house is clad with sunshades that allow constant air movement throughout. The pool is located under a triple-volume void that is punctuated by a network of ramps and bridges.

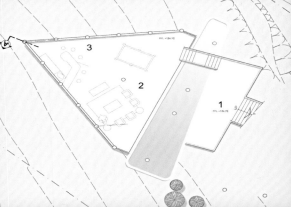

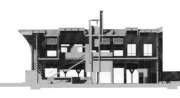

### Site 4 (LSD/NY)
A house in the middle of the woods with living spaces that bridge in and out with terraces and highly operable walls.

**Site 5 (LSD/NY)**
The green roof of this house, which commands a magnificent long view,
extends the ground plane of the entry grade with residential spaces below.

**Site 6 (LSD/NY)**
Located on a steeply sloping site with panoramic views, the structure is
elevated on stilts both to take in vistas and to allow ventilation from all sides.

## Site 7 (LSD/NY)

Embedded in the side of a small ravine, this elongated house looks through dense woods down a hill to a working paddy field.

## Site 8 (LSD/NY)

Near the centre of the plantation with glimpses through the trees of distant hills, the building is organised in three pavilions – linked via external walkways – centred on a pool and topped by a single sinewy roof.

Text © 2007 John Wiley & Sons Ltd. Images: pp 84-5, 87(b), 88-9 © Michael Sorkin Studio; pp 86, 87(t) © Jimmy Lim

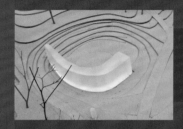

# Bangalore
# Architects

What Ahmedabad was for the architectural culture of India in the 1960s and 1970s, Bangalore is now in present times. A fortuitous combination of patronage and the presence of key architects produced a climate of innovative and imitable Modern architecture in Ahmedabad. A new form of patronage and investment has now catapulted the once bucolic city of Bangalore into the capital of 'India, Inc', a global buzzword for India's new economic turn. The resulting building boom has released an architectural energy that is evident in the plethora of work that showcases experiments and innovations in design.

The practice in Bangalore is also fraught with a paradox. Bangalore was once a city with a 'background' architecture, as Prem Chandavarkar describes in his earlier essay in this issue (see also the essay by Anuradha Mathur and Dilip da Cunha on the various landscape enterprises of Bangalore), where architecture was employed more towards the obligations of habitation and well-being than to a spectacular presence. This was perhaps a key reason why Bangalore did not fare prominently in the architectural history of modern India, being marginalised by the more extrovert and savvy Delhi-Ahmedabad-Mumbai axis. The sudden move into the spotlight in the age of euphoria for which Bangalore is a synonym creates a new challenge for the architecture of 'background'. In this double-edged condition, Chandavarkar also argues in his essay for the architects of Bangalore to adopt a critical practice, reflective and even slightly resistive, and insists on the need for not mere novelty but innovation, and the production of buildings not as billboards but as places of habitation.

The work in Bangalore is represented by a diverse group of architects and landscape architects operating with equally diverse orientations. Featured here are the projects of a selected few: Mathew & Ghosh Architects, Hundredhands, Chandavarkar and Thacker, Mindspace (Sanjay Mohe) and InFORM Architects (Kiran Venkatesh). The projects of Mathew & Ghosh and Chandavarkar and Thacker are particularly compelling. Mathew & Ghosh extend a Modernist idiom within a specific cultural complexity seen in a state of irreparable fissures to which architecture can respond only through a tenuous bricolage of shards and fragments. Chandavarkar and Thacker seek a 'negotiated practice' where the dilemma of spectacularity and habitation is mediated by 'an aesthetics of absorption', where a building is inclined towards absorbing and accruing meaning rather than flaunting it. They are joined by transnational architects whose work also contributes to the debate on design (for example, Michael Sorkin from New York and Jimmy Lim from Kuala Lumpur – see Sorkin's essay earlier in this issue). The work of other architects such as Shibanee & Kamal, Architecture Paradigm, Rajesh Renganathan and Vijay Vivek Shankar, no matter what positions they are taking – collaborative, innovative or resistive – add to the panorama of a dynamic architectural production that has only just begun.

# Mathew & Ghosh Architects

The work of Mathew & Ghosh Architects (Nisha Mathew-Ghosh and Soumitro Ghosh) boldly extends an abstract Modernist language and at the same time draws from the vitality of places. While the firm's early works were small in scale, mostly residential in nature and based on a reappraisal of the early Corbusian idiom, recent projects include large-scale urban and landscape interventions with diverse conceptual and metaphorical imperatives. They have moved from a more reticent stance to the urban exuberance of their more recent projects (for example, their own office building), something akin to a 'savage architecture' as posited by Kazuo Shinohara in the context of the unsynchronised nature of the modern city.

The architects' object of contemplation is the urban 'box', whether a private residence, office or part of a church. The box is first fractured and reconstructed as a bricolage of tectonic fragments, memories and events, all tenuously related as if unity in a contemporary culture is for ever denied. Like the Japanese notion of '*ma*', the moment between fragments – a slit or an emptiness between two hovering planes – is telling. Mathew & Ghosh participate in the continuity of a historical narrative yet mark out the fissures and disjunctions; sometimes negotiations with the continuity emerge from unintended interstices.

While these configurations of the contemporary urban 'box' are both contextual and abstract, they are also phenomenologically rich. There is a sustained dialect to the architecture of Mathew & Ghosh that includes consummate materiality and fine crafting, light as a medium, and always, as Nisha Mathew-Ghosh states, 'good spatial possibilities'.

## Mathew & Ghosh office and design studio, Bangalore, 2004

Multiple programmes and desires, both cross-referential and contradictory, organise the spatial and volumetric assemblage of this structure on a small site in a neo-urban location in Bangalore. A basic vertical division of a lower residential level for parents and an upper level for an architectural design studio leads to an essay on interpersonal and urban relationships.

While the parents' lower house retreats from the street, the upper 'house' accommodates the son's design studio in a set of exuberant, concatenated forms, made sometimes in concrete and sometimes wrapped in a sheath of metal. The assemblage includes 'tube' spaces for the design studio and private work space that is directed towards the street, reinforcing the desire to be involved with the public sphere, and in contrast to the retracted nature of the lower house.

## Benjamin House, Bangalore, 2001

Described as a 'house of fragments', the project highlights the exploration of the contemporary urban house, in this case the house as a linear space that is then reconfigured by conceptual spatial elements and the exigencies of site. While the street side is expressed as a stark wall, a private world is articulated behind it, with a verandah looking into a private garden that translocates the verandah–street relationship of earlier houses. In the interior, Mathew & Ghosh play with juxtapositions of material transparency, translucence and occasional opaqueness, and deliberate 'ruptures' that evoke the condition of the fragments and memories that are all contemporary culture is left with.

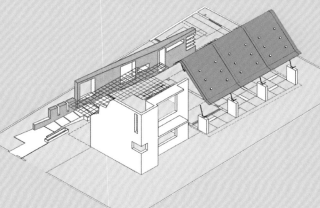

## SUA House corporate office, Bangalore, 2002

An essay on the urban box, in densely built-up conditions, the SUA office buildings stretch cheek by jowl, creating patterns through unintentional interstices of light and movement. This initially accidental interstitial space then becomes a deliberate player in organising the hierarchy of the office structure. Within the urban box, a private realm opens itself selectively to the outside, and as the clouds go by the building takes on innumerable nuances of sunlight, the different greys of the clouds and hues of the rainbow.

## St Mark's Cathedral Resource Centre, Bangalore, 2006

In the heart of the city, this resource centre for St Mark's Cathedral (which is 200 years old) houses miscellaneous activities such as Bible classes, training and youth programmes, computer training, a pastoral committee meeting hall, an auditorium to seat 200, a pastors' office and ancillary facilities. It was created by adding to and enveloping the shell of the 80-year-old parish hall, the most important part of which was retained by floating the new structure above the old. The new inserts and additions are differentiated from the old in terms of their language and articulation, and this is further reinforced by the physical separation of the two.

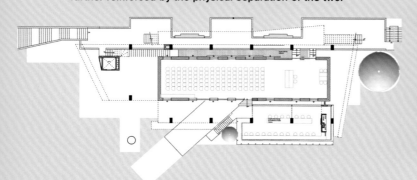

## Freedom Park, Bangalore, 2003

Mainly a landscaping project that opens up the prospect for a structured urban narrative, the Freedom Park (winner of a national competition to redevelop the site of the Old Central Jail of 1857) lies on the main north–south axis between Bangalore's Old Fort and the Palace. The general strategy here is to strengthen points along the axis to recognise the identities of historic Bangalore through instructive re-creations and interventions.

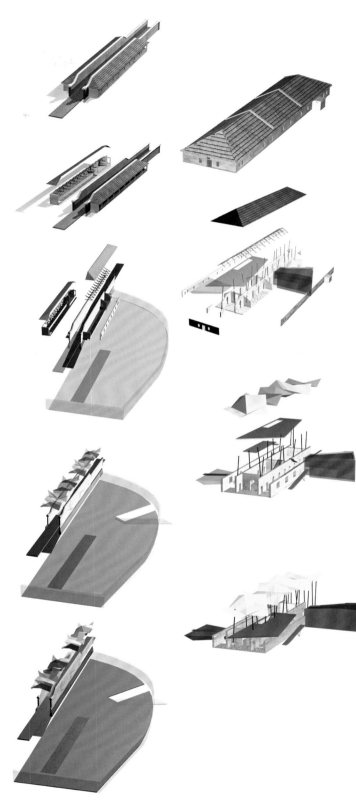

## Kuruvila House, Bangalore, 2002

On a tight suburban site, this private residence explores the spatial possibility of the enclosed verandah. The new space, conceived of as a 'verandah in the landscape' and enclosed for private living, responds to the movement of the sun and the breeze.

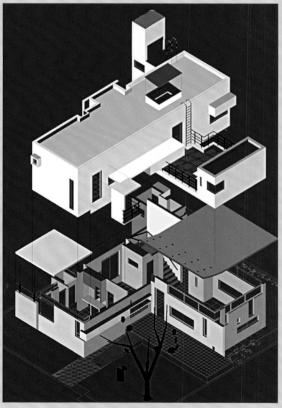

## Bhopal Gas Tragedy Victims Memorial Competition, 2005 (Awarded Second Position)

This memorial for the victims of the Union Carbide Bhopal Methyl Isocyanate gas tragedy of 1984 at the plant in Bhopal tests the notions of pain and healing. The disturbed 'brownfield' that needs to be cleaned before the site can be restored for public use led to the idea of a restorative and resurrective landscape, both literally and memorially. The new and revised landscape retains the scars of the tragedy and makes clearings between propped and hovering fragments that help make and negotiate the experience.

## Trinity – Malabar Escapes at Stuber Hall, Fort Cochin, Kerala, 2004

Developed in collaboration with Goetz Hagmuller of Kathmandu, Trinity – Malabar Escapes at Stuber Hall is an exercise in creating an 'authentic' contemporary Indian design that reflects upon the present time, location and context, as well as a sense of space and light, within the equally authentic yet older structure that encapsulates it.

In the 1740s, the Stuber Hall was the residence of the Viceroy of the Dutch East India Company. A heritage building in an important location next to the sea, the new addition is a hotel with three exclusive suites, a communal lobby and a dining/informal area along with a small pantry/service area. The architects have here combined contemporary Indian design with a clear Kerala experience – of the rain, humidity, sun and light, and of living in semicovered yet open areas. Thus the traditional Kerala home, with its courtyard which brings the rain into the centre of the home, was the starting point for the design of the new addition. Each room is a covered and enclosed space with an attic, a semicovered sitting area and outdoor bathing/ablution space that is really open to the surrounding natural greenery.

The hotel has a clear identity in that it plugs into the old structure without replicating traditional building characteristics: for example, some of the objects and furniture are authentic old Dutch pieces while others are modern Indian designs. In addition, where they remained undamaged, the existing *mangalore* tiles (top and underlay) were reused, with new tiles added only where they ran short, and the wood in the trusses was reconditioned with cashew oil (a dark brown colour) to protect it from termites and moisture. The false ceiling, which hid the trusses and roof, was removed completely to reveal the beauty of the roof form, its space and construction.

Text © 2007 John Wiley & Sons Ltd. Images: pp 92, 94(br), 95, 96(t), 97(b) © Mathew & Ghosh Architects Private Ltd, photos Soumitra Ghosh; p 93(t) © Mathew & Ghosh Architects Private Ltd, photo Mallikarjun Katakol; pp 93(b), 94(bl), 96(b), 97(t) © Mathew & Ghosh Architects Private Ltd; p 94(t) © courtesy Mathew & Ghosh Architects Private Ltd

# Hundredhands

Directed by Sunitha Kondur and Bijoy Ramachandran, Hundredhands is a multidisciplinary design studio whose work draws on a keen sense of the urban. In their projects, often represented in patiently executed analytical drawings, the architects have redirected their focus on the urban context by returning to questions of scale, character, spatial and visual impact, and remaking the public domain, all of which is so vital to the tempestuous urbanism of Indian cities.

## Raja ra Mane, Bangalore, 2005–

On a tight urban site, this nine-room boutique hotel is designed around a series of open-air spaces including a public restaurant patio off the street, a semipublic central court, and a private rear yard. These open spaces can be seen from the street, which creates a surprising porosity that is in contrast to the immediate context. The scale of the building here responds to the scale of the surrounding residential fabric.

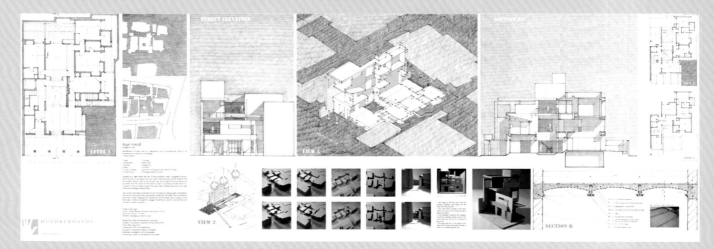

## The Center of HOPE, Tiruchchirapalli, Tamil Nadu, 2005

A residential facility for orphans, the centre also accommodates a 300-seat multipurpose hall, a dining facility, a public service dispensary with a laboratory and pharmacy, and classrooms for vocational training. The design responds to the climate and context of Tiruchchirapalli, the fourth largest city in the southern Indian state of Tamil Nadu, with its rich architectural legacy.

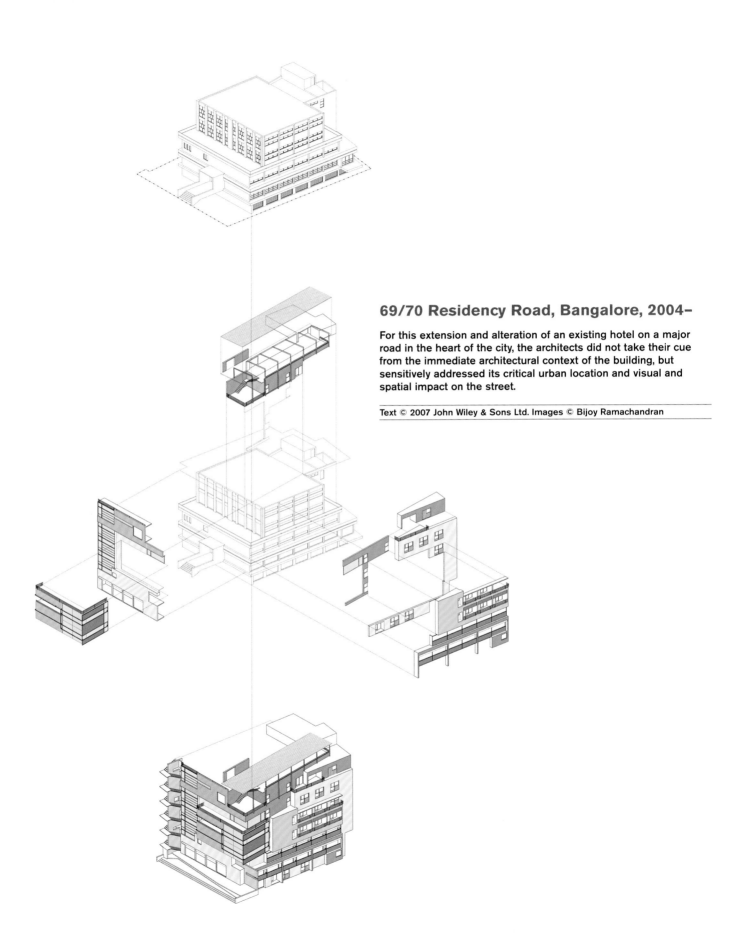

## 69/70 Residency Road, Bangalore, 2004–

For this extension and alteration of an existing hotel on a major road in the heart of the city, the architects did not take their cue from the immediate architectural context of the building, but sensitively addressed its critical urban location and visual and spatial impact on the street.

Text © 2007 John Wiley & Sons Ltd. Images © Bijoy Ramachandran

# Chandavarkar and Thacker

The first architectural firm in Bangalore, founded in 1947 by Narayan Chandavarkar, Chandavarkar and Thacker is currently under the directorship of Prem Chandavarkar and Sai Shankar Bharatan. Continuing the collaborative nature of the practice during its many reorganisations over the years, Prem Chandavarkar has also given the firm a new intellectual edge by confronting Bangalore's new urbanity, and as such is a role model for many younger-generation architects. The practice's current work represents thoughtful and reflective responses as architecture finds itself at a critical juncture in this city of a euphoric present.

With the practice's 60-year history, Chandavarkar is particularly aware of the humility and 'backgroundness' that once characterised the culture of the city in contrast to the present voluble environment. He has written (including in his essay in this issue) about the nature of practice and production, and has argued why a critical and self-reflexive practice needs to be the order of the day.

Chandavarkar and Thacker speak of an 'aesthetics of absorption' and a 'negotiated practice', both of which should inform a much needed criticality of the exuberant conditions today. 'A building does not convey meaning as much as it slowly absorbs it,' declares the practice, and so the test of a building is not the initial impression of its spectacular presentation, but the accrued experiences and memories of its everyday inhabitation. In their understanding of culture as an active and ongoing phenomenon, and hence one not yet susceptible to definition, the architects bring an open-endedness to their own practice. The result is an avoidance of a predetermined language of expression, and thus the variety of spatial, volumetric, site and technofunctional responses, in their array of works.

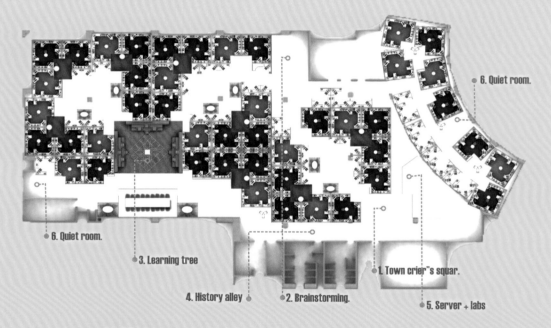

6. Quiet room.

6. Quiet room.

3. Learning tree

4. History alley

2. Brainstorming.

1. Town crier"s squar.

5. Server + labs

**Facilities**

Spatial hierarchy

## Office interior for MindTree Consulting, Bangalore, 1999

In the interior design of a six-storey, 1,400-person facility for an innovative IT organisation, the repetition of a basic work group creates spatial order at varying scales. The artwork for the project was contributed by the Spastic Society of Karnataka.

# Flower Auction Complex, Bangalore, 2006

This auction complex facilitates the export trade in cut flowers. Given the rocky nature of the eucalyptus-wooded site and the large volumes and scale of required spaces, the primary concern was to avoid making too harsh an imposition here. The architectural expression is inspired by the exactitude and pristine form of a flower hovering above the ground, and angled berms and cantilevered decks are used to diminish the sense of walls so that the triangulated white metal roof-forms float between the trees above the contours of the site.

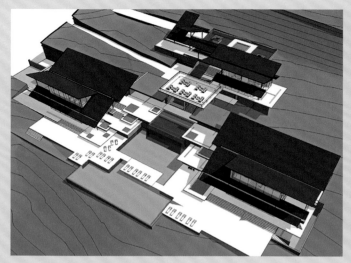

## Hill Resort, Chikmagalur, 2007

In this winning entry in a design competition for a resort on an unusual and dramatic site, the view down the exceedingly steep slope creates a sense of hovering, where the presence of human habitation in the valley below seems removed. From below, the view upwards creates a sense of the earth sweeping dramatically up towards a rugged cliff where one is acutely aware of the sky.

The design avoids the clichéd resort approach of packaged ethnicity and seeks a contemporary expression through amplifying the relationship with earth and sky. Buildings are carefully located to preserve the site's natural topography, vegetation and water run-off pattern. The architecture is visualised as a set of floor and roof planes that hover over the site, heightening the sense of dislodgement from the earth while preserving and sustaining the awareness of the topography.

# Biotech Innovation Centre, Hyderabad, 2007

The project responds to a complex technical programme for laboratory spaces, yet provides a spatial order for a vibrant research community. The spaces are divided around three nuclei that are linked by a spatial sequence. The first nucleus is contemplative in nature and houses an exhibition space showing the company's achievements. Envisaged as the 'jewel in the crown', this space is set within a reflecting pond. The second nucleus is a technical atrium that acts as a gathering space for scientists as they emerge from the laboratories, and the third is a social space surrounded by the cafeteria, recreation room and a mini-auditorium with a guesthouse above.

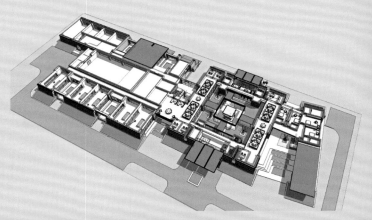

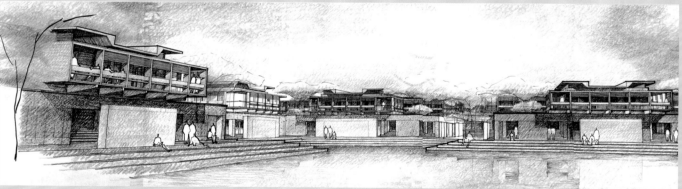

## College and School of Nursing, Apollo Hospitals, Chennai, 2004–

The design for this institution is based on a philosophy of the campus as a social community. The academic block of the campus is located on ground that slopes to a low point in the northeast corner where a rain-water harvesting pond is planned. The appearance from the water's edge evokes an Indian fort with walls at the lower levels and articulated pavilions at the higher level.

The hostel block accommodates 1,000 nurses and is developed in a pattern whereby the rooms look on to introverted secure courtyards that are gathering spaces for leisure and play.

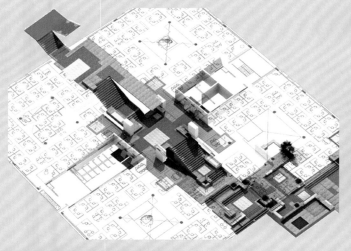

## ValueLabs Software Campus, Hyderabad, 2006

The challenge here was to create a friendly work environment within a relatively small site (0.8 hectares/2 acres) for a large workforce of 1,500. A sense of the larger community and the corporate image of the company were also important. Additionally, the project needed to adhere to the requirements of *vaastu* (the traditional principles of geomantic planning), which stipulated a square building with no offsets or projections.

Two major axes within the building split the plan into four quadrants. One axis houses services and elevators, while the cross axis, as a stepped street, unifies all the upper levels. This multivolume stair in the manner of a Gujarati stepped well forms a pedestrian walk vertically through the building and creates a community street giving a larger sense of 'campus'.

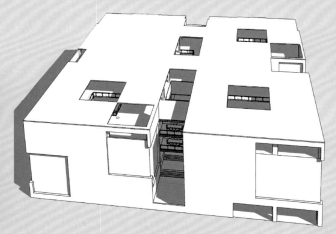

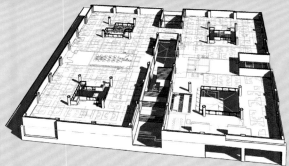

## Rubix commercial complex, Bangalore, 2007

In this proposal for a mixed-use iconic tower on a triangular site at the junction of major roads, the lower triangular podium houses retail and restaurant spaces connected to public plazas along the street edge. From the road, the pedestrian plaza reaches up to a neighbourhood park at the second-floor podium level. The upper office tower is divided into segments that twist as they rise.

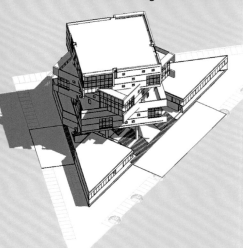

Text 2007 John Wiley & Sons Ltd. Text © 2007 John Wiley & Sons Ltd. Images © Chandavarkar & Thacker Architects Private Limited

# Mindspace (Sanjay Mohe)

The work of Sanjay Mohe, a former director with the firm of Chandavarkar and Thacker, represents the architectural ethos of Bangalore that mediates between a modulated Modernism and the contingencies of the city's specificities.

## Office for Bharatiya Reserve Bank Note Mudran, Bangalore, 2003

In this project, which Mohe designed as a director of Chandavarkar and Thacker, an opaque and sculpturesque exterior made of overlapping concrete panes is strikingly counterpoised by an inner atrium that opens out to a garden. The design for this corporate office for Bharatiya Reserve Bank Note Mudran Ltd – the official supplier of currency notes to the Bharatiya Reserve – was prompted by images of bank notes being counted by machines and whirring in the pattern of a fan deck, which was interpreted in the building as overlapping planes that make up the facade.

On approaching the building, which is surrounded by roads on three sides, one is presented with a series of overlapping portal frames along the north–south axis, with the entrance portals bending towards the gateway to envelop the visitor. Sheer blank walls along the peripheries block the traffic noise on the east and cut down the strong solar radiation on the west. The large garden lies to the south, separating the offices from a seven-storey building nearby.

Text © 2007 John Wiley & Sons Ltd. Images © Courtesy Mindspace

# InFORM Architects (Kiran Venkatesh)

**Kiran Venkatesh, as co-founder of InFORM Architects, faces head-on what he describes as paradigm shifts in the social and cultural patterns of India, and it is this that informs his architecture. Unlike the overall trend of arbitrary and whimsical responses, his sharply profiled and modulated forms continue to investigate such shifts as well as their spatial manifestation.**

## Tillany Fine Arts Museum and Gallery, Baliganapalli, Tamil Nadu, 2000

The purpose of this museum is to promote and display the work of talented artists and artisans from poorer backgrounds. On a tabula-rasa site, a regular Cartesian grid is subjected to local deformations to generate three separate bars. The central bar is a 12-metre (40-foot) high skylit atrium with two interlocked flights of stairs, and the floors on the two side bars are galleries for exhibiting the artwork.

The plan is interwoven with a section that enables the bars to have varying heights and widths. Here one is constantly aware of the changing relationship between body and building – sometimes the space narrows and at other times it widens, sometimes it is short and at other times very high. Movement from one bar to another is via bridges in the atrium; thus there are no closed rooms here, only spaces demarcated by voids and changes in passage widths. The grand stairs in the atrium as well as the connecting bridges also enable the artwork to be viewed from different vantage points.

## The Indian Institute of Journalism and New Media (IIJNM), Bagalur, Tamil Nadu, 2000

The IIJNM is devoted to the research and study of new media as well as more traditional forms such as newsprint, radio and so on. Set on a 1.2-hectare (3-acre) green-valley site, the campus is a network of interaction spaces that encourage debate among students and faculty. The institute's entire programme is organised formally along elongated bars that cross over one another in the form of a 'Y'.

## GRS Residence, Bangalore, 2004

On a 15.8 x 34 metre (52 x 112 foot) oblong site, the house is organised along a linear spine running parallel to a strip garden. The client had requested that the project strictly adhere to the predetermined methods of *vaastu* (the traditional principles of geomantic planning), and the architects cleverly used this as a design parameter to develop the highly structured organisation of the house. Here, the section is used to recast notions of domestic space – to reveal the existence of inner private spaces (for example, the bedroom box floating over the living room, resting on an orange column) without compromising their functionality. These pulsating volumes are composed in a three-dimensional space and plugged in to the central spine, creating a fluid and indeterminate internal space with an austere exterior surrounded by greenery.

A single orange-coloured textured wall runs the length of the site, making its appearance at different stages along the spine.

Text © 2007 John Wiley & Sons Ltd. Images: p 108 © InFORM Architects, photos S Vishwanath; p 109 InFORM Architects, photos Clare Arni

# Sharifa's House

In Bangladesh, a microbanking system exclusively targeted at female 'entrepeneurs' has been combined with a streamlined domestic construction process, transforming the possibilities of affordable housing for the rural poor. **Dr Adnan Morshed** tells Sharifa's story: how a very modest loan from the Grameen Bank allowed Sharifa and her family to build a house and to realise what amounts to very much more than even a permanent home.

Sharifa was a poor rural woman in Bangladesh. Her body language changed as her economic condition improved. She even bought herself some gold jewellery, an unthinkable investment for a village woman who possessed virtually nothing of any worth a year ago.

Some years ago, Sharifa, a poor woman in a village on the outskirts of Dhaka, received a meagre loan from the Grameen Bank, the Bangladesh-based microfinance organisation now well known around the world. With a lending philosophy hinged on the trustworthiness of the downtrodden, the Grameen Bank offers microcredit to the rural poor who typically do not have access to conventional banking. Upon receiving the Grameen microcredit, Sharifa bought two cows and started a small family business selling cow milk in a nearby bazaar. With the help of her two teenage daughters she milked the cows and employed her husband to sell the dairy product in the mostly male-dominated local market. Married off early, Sharifa was hardly educated, but her entrepreneurial drive and disciplined management of her business produced stunning results.

Although Sharifa's success sounds like a third-world version of the clichéd rags-to-riches narrative, the novelty of the story lay in her new awareness of domestic space as a fundamental condition for the social wellbeing of her family. In the subsistence economy of rural Bangladesh, investment in shelter for the poor is often viewed as unproductive, and hence conventional banks eschew housing loans to the rural poor. However, thanks to a Grameen Bank housing loan

received once Sharifa fruitfully invested her first loan and her credibility was established, Sharifa embarked upon a sublime journey from a poverty-stricken thatch-roofed house to a well-organised bungalow buttressed by reinforced concrete pillars and capped by corrugated-tin sheets.

Conventional wisdom would put Sharifa's humble new house squarely into the so-called fringe category Bernard Rudofsky has called 'architecture without architects'. In the 1960s Rudofsky championed vernacular architecture as a subject worthy of scholarly investigation, yet the discussion of vernacular environment remains entrenched in a false romance of timelessness. In contrast, Sharifa's architectural odyssey provides an insight into the dynamic ways the vernacular intersects with the modern market economy. Her rural cottage suggests not a radical formal departure from the traditional model, but rather a shift in the economy and efficiency of construction, and in the notions of durability, spatial arrangement and, most importantly, female participation in the production of space.

The Grameen Bank was initiated in Bangladesh in 1976 by the 2006 Nobel Peace Prize winner, economist Muhammad Yunus, to provide collateral-free microloans to poor rural communities for small businesses. Streamlining the

Next to her ornate new house, Sharifa's old house made with bamboo, clay and thatch stands as a silent vestige of her past destitution.

The new house signals the shifts in the ways rural architecture participates in microcredit-driven economy and new modalities of construction. A new awareness of durability underpins the construction process.

forbidding legal bureaucracy affiliated with conventional banking, the bank gradually sought to engage the vast female population, an untapped human resource in a predominantly male-centric and labour-intensive agrarian economy. If entrepreneurship was inspired among this potential group, the Bank believed, the effect would be far-reaching: financially independent, self-respecting mothers who would not only rear healthy, educated children for a better future, but also enlarge the national economy. Despite allegations of high interest rates and repressive loan recovery policies, the Grameen Bank has steadily staged a social revolution in rural Bangladesh.

Once the Grameen Bank's subsidiary operation – the Grameen Housing Loan Program – had developed, it became abundantly clear that better housing contributes to richer mental health, which in turn enhances productivity and

creativity. Therefore, contrary to the prevailing banking wisdom, investment in housing for the poor is prudent.

A housing loan requires that the recipient be a general borrower of the Grameen Bank, essentially making the rural women the exclusive target group of the housing loan. By virtue of this clause, the female borrower owns the house. The deed of proprietorship, on the one hand, provides considerable social leverage to the wife as her husband can no longer threaten her with an instant divorce – a common social vice in rural Bangladesh, though

The reinforced-concrete columns were initially mass-produced by the Grameen Bank itself for its borrowers, but later, when a sizable market for prefab pillars developed, many village-based industries with the technical know-how emerged and met the market demands swiftly and efficiently.

fortunately there are signs that it is decreasing. Owning a property gives her a familial status of indispensability. In addition, it bestows crucial decision-making power in planning the new house on her.

A maximum of US$236 is sanctioned as a housing loan to be repaid over a period of five years in weekly instalments. The Grameen officials usually advise the female borrower on construction, building materials, and how to make the house durable. But in the end, how the dwelling will be built is her call. While it follows the archetypal morphology of a rural house consisting of a simple rectangular plan with pitched roof, the Grameen house replaces corner wooden posts – susceptible to termites and flooding – with prefabricated reinforced-concrete columns that are available in the local market. Employing local construction crews as well as

*Far left:* Female borrowers await the disbursement of loans at a rural Grameen Bank branch.

*Left:* The private bathroom, with a deep well and attached to the main house, is both a convenience and a trope of prosperity.

investing her own household labour, the borrower can erect the skeleton of the house on a protective plinth in a matter of days. Unlike the traditional model, the new construction includes a sanitary latrine – a modular prefab reinforced-concrete toilet pan with a water seal, enclosed in a tin shade, that ensures privacy for family members. A new streamlined construction process significantly alters the way the poor rural community conventionally understands the concept of a shelter and, ultimately, its purposes and potentials.

The basic structure of a typical Grameen house can be built expeditiously.

For the poor borrower, the skeletal form of the house becomes a tabula rasa for all kinds of social projections and imaginations, collectively negotiating the overarching idea that spatial organisation and its visual representation can also be potent tools for social mobility. The durability of the house, then, is no longer just the protective denomination of the enclosure; rather, durability in this context takes on a broadened cultural definition, one that articulates the Grameen borrower's yearning for dignity.

Sharifa's house is a strong case in point. The spatial arrangement that grows out of the basic module transcends mere utilitarian needs and bears the imprints of Sharifa's new self-conscious persona. Formerly unknown or ignored, privacy is now ensured as two bedrooms are planned – one for her and her husband, and the other for the daughters. Her abode calibrates the spatial layout with the diverse needs of the family.

The decoration pieces, the showcase and the wall hangings that adorn the bedroom are indices of the family's economic growth as well as the feminisation of the basic module. The television primarily serves entertainment purposes, yet it is also a metaphor for the family's desire to outgrow minimal existence. The wall clock is not just a timepiece, but a signifier of Sharifa's attempt to restructure her life around standard time rather than a personal one, a temporal readjustment that is crucial for an efficient management of her business. Her daughters' room and the wall hangings in it – from badminton racket to Miss Universe – cast long shadows of middle-class aspirations.

Although a single-floor house would have sufficed, Sharifa's two-storeyed bungalow suggests a kind of 'social towering' in the blighted landscape of poverty. The bright colours of the walls, the protective grill and the decorative pediment adorning the roofline buttress a longing for social prestige. The loggia at the second level is the metaphoric incorporation of the gaze of the *zamindar*, or landed gentry, from the *piano nobile* of his mansion that grants him a synoptic view of his property. With startling sophistication Sharifa crafts an architectural language that bespeaks her intended emigration to middle-class life.

Sharifa's house does not imply the loss of traditional spatiality; rather, we witness tradition's enriching

The 'height factor' in Sharifa's two-storeyed bungalow is less about a real need for space than about the family's yearning for social visibility. Although an elevated verandah overlooks the surrounding landscape, the first floor is used mostly for storage.

intersection with modernity and its attendant norms of efficiency and economic management. But what it shows, more importantly, is that the primal form of tradition morphs into a crucial site for fashioning an identity based on self-esteem, thanks to microcredit-based entrepreneurships. The structural durability of Sharifa's Grameen house also reveals the durability of a new kind of matriarchal family values that emerge out of the rural women's attempt to outpace social anonymity. However, the formation of such values is not without friction, and necessarily excludes the husband from the equation. Despite the tension resulting from the shift in family power hierarchy, the new-found financial security enables a new type of bonding between the borrower and her husband, based on the shared dream of a better future.

It would be premature, though, to surmise that social empowerment is an easy objective that could be achieved by dutifully subscribing to the vision of the Grameen Bank. An understanding of Sharifa's new-found confidence in shaping both her social and physical space requires a probing look into the very concept of empowerment and its relationship to gender justice.

The 1998 Economics Nobel Laureate Amartya Sen's ideas of women's proactive self-representation shed light on the idea of empowerment. In an active condition, a woman speaks for herself, and has the ability to shape her own destiny the way

The poster of the Bollywood superstar and former Miss Universe Aishwarya Rai adorns the wall of Sharifa's daughters' bedroom.

Marked by an assortment of posters, decorative objects, a wall clock and a television, the interior of Sharifa's house is an embodiment of middle-class dreams.

Sharifa and her daughters' outlook changed from despair to hope.

she deems fit, rather than being the passive recipient of a social programme that has already determined what is best or most suitable for her. Women's empowered condition, Sen observes, charts a shift from the initial focus exclusively on women's wellbeing to a more activist concentration on their right to self-representation. A 'welfarist' approach is ultimately premised on a flawed view of women as voiceless patients who just await care rather than women as agents of change. An agenda for women's empowerment, therefore, must ultimately envision women not simply as 'receivers', but as individuals with certain responsibilities and capabilities. In addition to seeking the basic wellbeing of women, an activist programme for women's agency must also acknowledge the social capital that is generated from their education, employment and entrepreneurship. What Sen suggests is that the battle for women's entitlement has to be fought not simply on the legislative front, but, more effectively, on multilateral social fronts that include education and broad public engagements with the issues of inequality.

Economists, social scientists and non-governmental organisations concerned with advancing women's issues have rightly emphasised the role of non-legislative social campaigns in fighting the root causes of women's exclusion from the discourses of power. But what they have typically missed pointing out is the enormity of the ways in which the production of domestic space might have broad ramifications for women's empowerment. As Sharifa's house reveals, architecture becomes a crucial addition to the list of social and economic variables that enhance both women's welfare and their ability to represent themselves. If the pursuit of women's agency is a protracted social battle, then that battle could well be fought – as in Sharifa's case – in making the house an extension of the empowered female self.

Sharifa's inspiring story, however, ends with a caveat. Architecture as an image of empowerment can also come at an environmental cost. Unlike the comfort ensured by traditional mud walls, the thermal performance of the corrugated-tin walls – the symbol of affluence – of the new house is ironically below acceptability, for tin causes excessive interior heat gain during summer and loss during winter. While physical durability and the social symbolism of women's empowerment could only enrich the new house, the success of the Grameen Housing Loan Program resides eventually in a meaningful synthesis of the empowerment factor and a researched consideration of eco-friendly building materials. ⌂

Text © 2007 John Wiley & Sons Ltd. Images © Adnan Morshed

# This is Not a Building!
## Hand-Making a School in a Bangladeshi Village

The opportunity to design a village school for an educational institute in northern Bangladesh, whose guiding tenet is 'learning with joy', provided European architects Anna Heringer and Eike Roswag with a unique commission. **Kazi K Ashraf** describes how this collaborative community effort has resulted in a wholly inventive and intriguing design, realised solely with traditional materials and local skills.

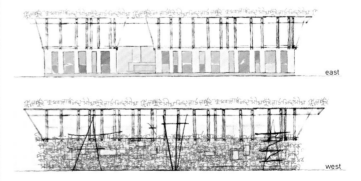

*Everybody learnt a lot from each other. I learned how to build strong walls, how to use measurement tools and the foreigners learnt that the best mixing machines are water buffalos.*

— Suresh, loam worker

The building – a school – is small and inconsequential in the scheme of things, with a modest footprint of 275 square metres (2,960 square feet), and located in a village called Rudrapur far in the north of Bangladesh, but it has already stirred fascination at many levels. Designed by Anna Heringer of Austria and Eike Roswag of Germany, the project received the Aga Khan Award for Architecture this year. Jurors at the 2007 Kenneth F Brown Asia-Pacific Architecture Award, who included Kerry Hill, Itsuko Hasegawa and the editor of the *Architectural Record,* Robert Ivy, anointed the project as a model for future developments. Ivy noted that the project quickly stood out because of the design quality achieved with minimum materials and as a programme that involved the community.

In the vast stretch of the South Asian rural milieu, where people are mostly left to fend for themselves regarding building, few examples abound with vitality as architectural energy orbits mostly the cities. In the passionate hands and minds of Heringer and Roswag, age-old building materials like bamboo, mud and even the fabric for saris, whose creative incarnation seems to have been exhausted, find a new delightful lease. The modest little school takes site and rural milieu one joyous degree further.

The architects describe the two-storey structure as being 'hand-made by local craftsmen, pupils and teachers together with a European team of architects, craftsmen and students'. The special school for village children is part of the Modern Education and Training Institute (METI) in Rudrapur, and the project was realised with support from the development agency Dipshikha, the Shanti Bangladesh Partnership Association and the Papal Children's Mission (PMK). The key philosophy of METI is learning with joy where the teachers facilitate the children in developing their own potential and using it in a creative and responsible way. The aim of the

**Anna Heringer and Eike Roswag, Hand-Made School for METI, Rudrapur, northern Bangladesh, 2006**
Children in the cave-like spaces in the ground floor. The soft interior of these spaces allows children to retreat into their own space or group for exploration or concentration, or just nestle up.

east

west

Exterior bamboo lattices are for growing vegetable vines as well as shading the building. In these elevation drawings, the architects have cleverly used the flowing Bengali script to name all the local vegetables.

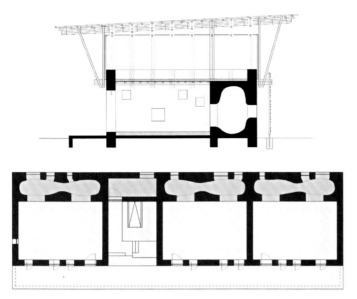

The ground floor is made of thick mud walls, while the upper floor is a porous, latticed space in bamboo.

school project was to improve existing building techniques, maintaining sustainability by utilising local potential and strengthening regional identity. The architects note: 'We are convinced that architecture means more than just satisfying a need for shelter. For us architecture and building is closely linked with the creation of identity and self-confidence. This is the basis for sustainable and forward-looking development.'

The compact and simple volume of the school does not immediately reveal its innovative conditions. The ground floor, with its thick earth walls, has three classrooms with organically shaped cave-like spaces to the rear of each. Formed by loam, the soft interiors of theses spaces are 'for touching, for nestling up against, for retreating into for exploration or concentration, on one's own or in a group'. The upper floor is by contrast airy and light, and presents sweeping views across the surroundings, beyond tree tops and the village pond to the paddy fields. The permeable walls on this floor are made of bamboo strips that cast playful light and shadows across the earth floor contrasting with the colourful saris used as canopies.

The use of earth and bamboo as building materials draws upon traditional building techniques, now imbued with technical improvements. The whole project is very much about the process: how locally available resources, abilities and labour were used to build cost-effective and better buildings, and how local labourers who took part in the construction were trained in improved building techniques. The schoolchildren and teachers were also integrated throughout the building process, thus contributing to the making of their own school (for example, the students made the straw-earth rolls for the door and window surrounds). The surfaces of the building also reflect the people within: the doors bear in Bengali the names of the children and will continue to be so inscribed as a chronology of the school.

Rural architecture in South Asia – and here is a compelling example from Bangladesh – could see a vitality too, and return to the precepts of sustainable and ecological design as a truly joyous and socially effective enterprise. The beauty of this hand-made structure is not only in the end building, however photogenic it may be, but in the process of its making, which emphasised the active and verbal nature of the term 'building', recalling both Gandhi's principles of making sustainable and ecological buildings, and the Egyptian architect Hasan Fathy's community activism. Embedded, like Fathy in the village of Gourna, Heringer and her companions basically arrived from the cosmopolis to renew the art of building for a somewhat atrophied tradition. While they may have started with an architectural upper hand (which might incite some postcolonial harangue), they also learned a few things along the way, about humility and humanity, and about the larger social impact of a modest building. Perhaps a bit asymmetrically, a conversation ensued that resulted in an enlightening project in materials innovation, community participation and technology transfer. The villagers have started to rediscover a depleted consciousness about their age-old building materials. Paul Tigga, the head of Dipshikha, notes: 'We can already sense the new-found enthusiasm and hope that building with earth can inspire for improving the quality of living for the poor in rural areas.' This may be affirmed by the hundreds of people from surrounding villages who throng to see the amazing little school in Rudrapur. ∆

**Article based on unpublished text and quotes provided by Anna Herringer**

## CONSTRUCTION

| | People | | Materials used |
|---|---|---|---|
| 8 | bricklayers | 83 | square metres (893 square feet) of masonry brickwork for the foundations and verandah |
| 12–20 | labourers for earthen building | | |
| 8 | labourers for bamboo construction | 270 | square metres (2,906 square feet) of cob for walls, ceilings in the 'caves' and rammed earth floors |
| 1 | foreman | | |
| 2 | apprentices and 5 trainees | 400 | tonnes wet earthen material |
| 5 | plasterers | 2,300 | bamboo canes for ceilings, upper storey and facades |
| 1 | local foreman | 12,500 | bamboo strips for upper storey bamboo facades |
| 2 | architects | | |
| 2 | crafts experts (team from Germany) | | Construction period: 5 months (September to December 2005) |
| 4–6 | volunteers (students, teachers, workmen from Germany and Austria) | | |

**Rudrapur, 9th October, 2005**
Finally, although we can still not see the sun, the heavy rainfall has subsided to a light drizzle. … We can begin to work again. Some of the workers arrive with their heads hanging low. The heavy rain has caused some of the dwellings to collapse and the condition of the houses is the main topic of conversation. Our project it seems has taken centre stage. To build a school and at the same time train 25 workmen is a good and important cause. However, to effect a fundamental improvement in the living conditions in such rural areas, we must develop and show further approaches that can be built by the population themselves. A transfer of knowledge and information is necessary in order to help the people become independent of materials and loans. During the day more visitors arrive at the building site than usual. The heated debate continues in the evening in the tea stall. Bankim, an old acquaintance from a Brahmin family, complains vehemently about how little the 'stupid earth' can withstand. His house also collapsed the night before after only eight years. His exclamations serve only to stimulate the discussion. 'Bankim, if you can't build properly, how can you fault the material?' Half-stung and taken aback by the young woman's retort, Bankim wades into the discussion with a BUT to counter each of my arguments. Cost-effectiveness is of little interest to those better off: 'Cost-effective is gut [sic], BUT better still is a house that doesn't fall down every few years'. 'It's all very well if its good for the environment BUT why is it down to me to …'. 'It may be that houses made out of earth are better to live in than brick houses, it may be that they don't get so hot, they don't rot so much, the food reserves hold longer … BUT how does that help me if I have to build a whole house again and again'. Bankim concords on only one argument: that the villages will lose their beauty and their face if houses were only built of bricks and tin roofs. BUT. Bankim won't be convinced too quickly. 'So, if it really is possible to make buildings out of earth that last ten times longer then that would be a major improvement. I will take a look at your tinkering about tomorrow when it's light … BUT be warned, I will check it very carefully.' The next day at half past eight, Bankim appears next to me on the wall, takes the spade from my hand and tries his luck. He trims the wall a little, checks the foundations, the damp-proof course, the straw-clay mixture. Finally he goes to his motorbike, mounts it, drives a few metres, then turns around grinning: 'Anna-Di, from today on there will be no more BUTs!'

**14th December, 2005**
The disc of the sun has now disappeared and only a golden-red stripe still glows over the horizon, the call of the Muezzin mingling with the song of the Hindu-women. Today a Muslim, a Hindu and a Christian priest have blessed the school with Sura, Mantras and Psalms. I hope with all my heart that despite the political tensions this school can remain a place of peace, of freedom and of dialogue.

Extracts from Anna Heringer's diary

Text © 2007 John Wiley & Sons Ltd. Images © Kurt Hoerbst, www.hoerbst.com

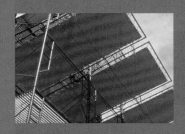

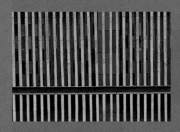

# Subcontinental Panorama

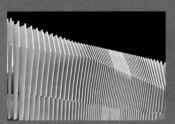

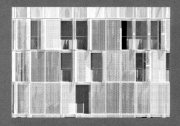

The Indian panorama is also intimately tied to the broader phenomenon of the subcontinent. As Qurratulain Hyder invokes in her 1957 novel *The River of Fire*, there is a fluid and porous nature to the reality of the subcontinent despite the forging of nationhoods and manning of borders. This is shared as much in the circulation of Bollywood Pop as in the production of architecture. Despite the sameness of a glib consumerism marked by luxury malls and raunchy residences, towards which many architects are understandably rushing, architecture in the subcontinent faces some formidable issues: How best to reconfigure the city, humanistically and ecologically, in the climate of rushed development? How to transform urban types for rising levels of middle-class requirements? How to mobilise the resources of the new economy to raise millions out of poverty? And, how to rephrase questions of identity and locality without being parochial or dogmatic?

Featured here is a group of projects from eastern India, Sri Lanka and Bangladesh that might be paradigms for building in a hot-humid milieu, in a landscape of vegetal and hydrological intensity. Theirs is an architecture of porosity sought in a language of walls that dissolve into lattices, brise-soleils, and various kinds of perforations and diaphanous membranes. This is represented in the work of Team Architrave (Madhura Prematilleke) and C Anjalendran of Sri Lanka; Shattoto: Architecture for Green Living (Rafiq Azam) of Bangladesh; as well as foreign architects Ann Pendleton-Jullian and Piercy Conner Architects & Designers. The apartment buildings in Dhaka by Rafiq Azam, while conforming to the metrical and fiscal requirements of the developer, have been able to introduce 'green' spaces in inventive ways at various levels as gardens in the air. The Govinda Gunalanker Hostel in Chittagong by Saif Ul Haque Sthapati, also featured here, is a strong demonstration of site relationship, community spaces and the translation of a historical typology. The work of the Singapore-based architect Kerry Hill, which deploys a material elegance and site responsiveness, offers a link to the broader pan-Asian tropical Modernism. Some of the projects of Studio Mumbai Architects (see 'Mumbai Architects' section), around humid Mumbai also share this language.

Despite the unmistakable urban upsurge and dynamic growth, a vast part of the subcontinent is rural, and remains yoked to the tribulations of both tradition and nature. Few architects have been able to articulate a point of engagement with the rural milieu, except during catastrophic moments such as earthquakes and tsunamis. The post-earthquake projects in Gujarat by Vastu Shilpa Consultants (see 'Material Formations' section) are an example of such an engagement. So are the Harvard Tsunami Design Initiative (TDI) safer houses for Sri Lanka. And the 'hand-made' mud school by Anna Heringer and Eike Roswag in a remote village in Bangladesh is an incredibly inspirational example of the cathartic capacity of architecture (see earlier essay by Kazi K Ashraf). The Grameen Housing Loan Program (see Dr Adnan Morshed's essay, also in this issue), not so much in the conventional language of architecture, and notwithstanding some of the criticisms of microcredit, affirms the social and gender impact of such building programmes.

# Kerry Hill Architects

With a practice based in Singapore and an office in Fremantle, Australia, Kerry Hill Architects has committed itself to creating innovative and regionally appropriate architecture and being in the vanguard of what has been considered a pan-Asian tropical Modernism. Hill has emerged as an influential figure in the architectural culture of Southeast Asia, and with a series of impressive awards the practice has produced distinguished resorts and city hotels, schools, recreational facilities and residential projects. According to Hill: 'The uniqueness of place must be allowed to surface – for architecture involves the actuality of things and speaks to the senses – it cannot rely on image alone.'

## Amankora, Bhutan, 2007

Amankora is a resort project in the small Himalayan kingdom of Bhutan where Kerry Hill is creating buildings that are Bhutanese in form, materiality and spirit. Prominent architectural features such as the use of stabilised earth, the roof structures, building forms and proportions are informed by traditional Bhutanese architecture. The interiors of the public areas and guest rooms also make reference to Bhutanese design, especially the varied and rich culture of indigenous weaving and dyeing processes.

The construction of the stabilised earth walls for Amankora is a refinement of the indigenous mud-building technique. Traditionally, earth from the site is poured into timber formwork and compacted using manually operated wooden rammers to form walls up to 0.6 metres (2 feet) thick that provide the outer shell of the building. The earth wall is then plastered with white lime to prevent it deteriorating over time. However, the construction of the buildings for the Amankora project involved mixing the earth with a carefully controlled percentage of cement and waterproofing additive. The earth mix was then poured into metal formwork and compacted in layers using mechanical rammers, and the exterior face treated with a waterproofing sealant.

Guest rooms are designed to act as cocoons, providing refuge from the Himalayan climate. All walls and ceilings are wrapped in local timbers. Floors throughout are finished in wide solid-timber boards, and window openings provide framed views of the forest and mountains beyond. Bathrooms are planned as integral to the living/bedroom area, with a centrally positioned fireplace inspired by the traditional *bukhari* (wood-burning stoves) of Bhutan.

## ITC Sonar Bangla Hotel, Kolkata, 2003

The ITC Sonar Bangla Hotel in Kolkata is an original re-interpretation of the liquid landscape of Bengal. While Kerry Hill has produced a number of striking hotel projects all over Asia that bear the recognisable marks of his design – elegant, Miesian planning with heightened material sensoriality and a relationship with the landscape – the Sonar Bangla Hotel is an original reinterpretation of the liquid landscape of Bengal. Hill has here turned an existing body of water on the site into the heart of the hotel complex, around which the public areas and hotel guest rooms are situated, offering an aesthetic interpretation of the aquatic, flood-prone landscape of the region. This is particularly remarkable when one considers that the design of gardens and grounds in most public buildings in India falls back on the predictable theme of the Mogul landscape with its geometric gardens and pools. Any essay on the architecture and landscape of the hot-humid aquatic milieu of Bengal also engages the pavilion paradigm – of the freestanding perforated structure in the landscape. The building masses of the hotel are fragmented but connected with courtyards and colonnades along the water spaces, and the lofty volumes of the tea pavilions on the water's edge are perforated for natural ventilation. Continuing his preoccupation with materials and crafting, Hill uses local glass-reinforced concrete louvres that are pigmented with brick dust and which, because of their imprecise, rusticated quality, add a hand-crafted feel.

Text © 2007 John Wiley & Sons Ltd. Images: p 120 © Courtesy of Amanresorts; p 121(bl) © Kerry Hill Architects, photo Patrick Bingham-Hall; p 120(t&br) © Kerry Hill Architects, photos Albert Lim KS

# Piercy Conner Architects & Designers

**Piercy Conner, an innovative practice based in London, extends the theory and practice of architecture in a way 'that demonstrates a profound understanding of its cultural and communicational possibilities', and is the firm behind a number of microflat projects in and around London.**

## SymHomes Mk1, Kolkata, 2006

Piercy Conner's winning entry for the Living Steel Rajarhat New Town competition met the brief of creating an alternative to conventional housing through the firm's steel kit of parts, described as 'an economically viable alternative: expressive, joyful and responsive to the environment'.

SymHomes Mk1, developed with Bengal Shrachi and Tata Steel, represents the symbiotic relationship of a sealed, conditioned, contemporary living space enveloped by a permeable responsive outer skin. This simple and robust strategy explores the closed nature of Western homes in contrast to the permeability of subtropical architecture and the tendency of the sealed box to prevail across the globe. As the skin becomes permeable, the in-between space becomes an outdoor room and the internal spaces engage with the landscape, expressed externally as a series of peeled-back layers. The outer patterned skin borrows from the expressive and permeable architecture of Kolkata and is also a direct result of the mapping of sun paths.

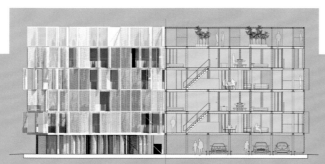

Text © 2007 John Wiley & Sons Ltd. Images © Piercy Conner Architects

# Shatotto: Architecture for Green Living (Rafiq Azam)

Rafiq Azam, based in Dhaka, Bangladesh, has produced interventionist architecture in Dhaka city's unchallenged urbanity where owner-developer profits tightly dictate the terms of engagement. His designs for apartment buildings are regarded as compelling revisions of given typologies. In his urban projects, Azam has dematerialised the obtrusive and anti-urban boundary wall that characterises the city with new layerings of gardens, plantings and other architectural fragments such as gardens in the air. His contribution to the 'greening' of apartments is original and clearly an achievement in the rigid mathematics of the market.

## Gulfeshan Apartment Building, Dhaka, 2003

The Gulfeshan apartment building is a 20-family housing complex near a lake to the east, and represents the juxtaposition of rural and urban landscape imageries.

## Meghna Residence, Dhaka, 2006

In an area undergoing a radical transformation from primarily two-storey single-family dwellings on open plots to six-storey multi-family complexes jostling against each other, the Meghna Residence is an obstinate oasis in the fast disappearing green and open spaces of the city. While the ground floor of this large house for a single extended family is devoted to services, the living areas are stacked vertically, with a swimming 'pond' on the roof deck acting as a landscaped ghat.

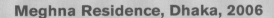

## Mizan Residence, Dhaka, 2004

Here, a six-storey apartment building on a lakeside becomes an instrument to re-establish relationships with the rhythms of nature. The focus and challenge of the project was to create a residence at the top of the building – realised in the form of an ingenious duplex space – where the Mizan family could enjoy the variegated conditions of seasonal changes and natural vegetation, and at the same time maintain their privacy.

Text © 2007 John Wiley & Sons Ltd. Images © Rafiq Azam, Shatotto

# Ann Pendleton-Jullian

Ann Pendleton-Jullian practises from Cambridge, Massachusetts, where she also teaches at MIT. This combination of teaching and practice allows her to consider the vital exchange between ideas and architecture that is evident in both her commissioned work and her theoretical projects. Her work has been cited for the manner in which it poeticises the intersection between pragmatic concerns and the 'ambitions of the imagination'.

## Access Program Buildings, Asian University for Women, Chittagong, Bangladesh, 2006

This design, initially proposed for the Access Program Buildings for the planned Asian University for Women on a vulnerable hilly terrain in the second largest city of Bangladesh, takes into account both topographical and ecological factors, and also offers a new model for grouping buildings in an academic 'village'. Pendleton-Jullian suggests 'garden', 'cloud', and 'inlay' as the organisers for this building group for the new university.

The garden is at the northwestern end of a long sinuous ridge, a terrace formed by cutting into the 67-metre (220-foot) contour line. The shape and articulation of its outline reveal the scale of the erosive forces operating on the soft geological material here. At the edge of the ridge, a building is formed by the placement of four pavilions – a classroom, IT centre, library and administration block – that cohere around a square courtyard, a place of stillness within the intense undulations of the landscape. This is what Pendleton-Jullian calls the 'cloud'. All this rests on an 'air plinth', and is wrapped in a protective casing that responds algorithmically to the changing parameters of solar orientation, wind directions and views in or out, revealed or veiled.

Finally, the housing is inlaid into the topography, hanging from the contour line. Organised as a chain, where the basic double dorm unit can be configured in various different ways to achieve increasing scales of interaction, the housing strands plait together to modulate the street and at the same time are themselves modulated by water courts fed from channels in the street.

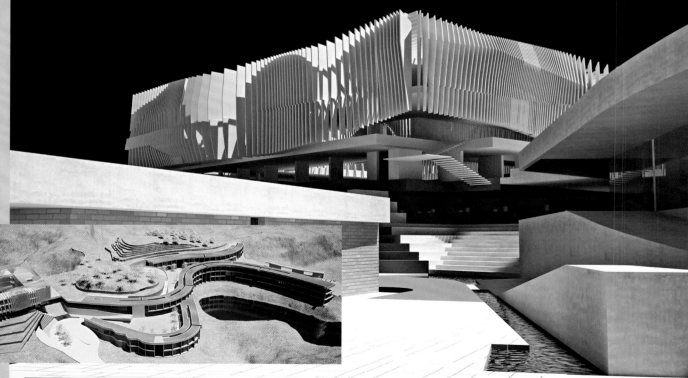

Text © 2007 John Wiley & Sons Ltd. Images © Ann M Pendleton-Jullian

# Saif Ul Haque Sthapati

Since establishing his practice in Dhaka in 1986, Saif Ul Haque has become an architectural provocateur in response to the urgency of place and time. As a prominent figure in the field of critical urban and environmental issues, he continues to produce original research and publications, as well as organising forums for young architects.

## Govinda Gunalanker Hostel, Chittagong, Bangladesh, 1998

This hostel for Buddhist students translates the historic typology of a traditional monastery into a modern student dormitory. The architect has here taken the rural or non-urban milieu as an arena for architectural interventions where traditional features such as the courtyard, grouping of buildings, siting and other architectural elements are realigned in contemporary terms.

Text © 2007 John Wiley & Sons Ltd. Images © Saif Haque Sthapati

# Tsunami Design Initiative (TDI)

TDI was formed by Ellen Chen, Eric Ho, Nour Jallad, Rick Lam and Ying Zhou of Harvard University and, with Michelle Addington as consultant, went on to win the Tsunami Challenge Competition in 2005, hosted by the MIT SIGUS group, which called for ideas for rebuilding efforts following the catastrophic tsunami in South Asia in 2004. In order to realise such a large project, the team needed to be expanded and the project was therefore carried out in collaboration with Luis Berrios, Justin Lee and Carlo Ratti (SENSEable City Laboratory, Cambridge, Massachusetts) and Walter Nicolino (carlorattiassociati, Turin, Italy), with Domenico Del Re (Buro Happold, London) as structural engineer.

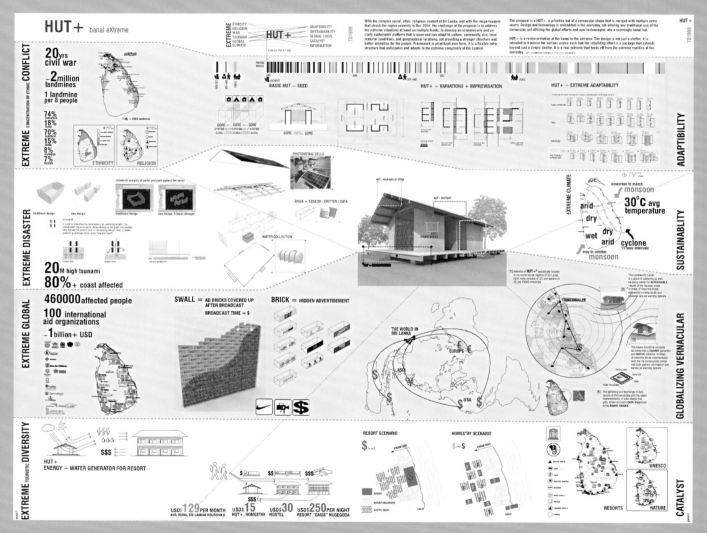

## Tsunami Safe(r) House, various sites, Sri Lanka, 2005–

The initial, competition-winning concept of a flexible-plan core-and-infill house that responds to local site conditions and is structurally sound was further developed in the Tsunami Safe(r) House and executed by the Prajnopaya Foundation (Massachusetts) and the Sri Bodhiraja Foundation. The first prototype of the house was completed in September 2005 in Balapitiya, Sri Lanka.

Text © 2007 John Wiley & Sons Ltd. Images © TDI

# Madhura Prematilleke (Team Architrave)

Madhura Prematilleke practises with his colleagues at Team Architrave in Colombo, Sri Lanka, and considers himself an Asian Modernist in search of what he calls a 'robust architecture' that 'can accommodate – and indeed thrive upon – the manner in which it is used, misused or otherwise "Asianised"'. This view of Modernism stems from the fact that, as Prematilleke explains, 'in a cultural landscape such as ours in Sri Lanka – where urban contexts are chaotic, tastes are wildly heterogeneous, and usage of buildings abrasive, Modernism, in particular, with its aspirations of purity and lucidity, is hardly able to cope'.

## Long House 1 (Chandan and Nadhini De Silva Residence), Colombo, 2003

Arranged on a long and narrow site, the main requirements for this residence were perfect ventilation and bright but sheltered spaces. A long garden and spine wall run the length of the house, and a circulation path weaves alongside the wall, emerging from the house as a bridge and concluding in steps leading down to the garden. The rooms are strung along the circulation path, culminating in a double-height living room.

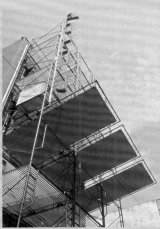

## Royal Bakery, Colombo, Sri Lanka, 1999

The inspiration for this prolific city bakery (a neighbourhood institution for almost a century) came from a typically Sri Lankan building type – the ubiquitous *kadé*, or wayside boutique, which, with its wooden shutters removed, is completely open with no facade, and spills out on to the street. In this case a screen was introduced to the facade-less building in the form of a permanent scaffold, its numerous canopies and pergolas creating a means of shade and shelter, while at the same time retaining the transparent nature of the building.

Text © 2007 John Wiley & Sons Ltd. Images: p 127(t) © Eresh Weerashriya; p 127(b) © Madhura Prematilleke

# Contributors

**Kazi K Ashraf** teaches at the University of Hawaii School of Architecture. He studied at MIT and the University of Pennsylvania. He writes on phenomenological issues of architecture and landscape, and contemporary South Asia. He co-edited the publication *An Architecture of Independence: The Making of Modern South Asia* (Architectural League of New York, 1997), and has curated exhibitions on Modern architecture in South Asia, Louis Kahn's Capital Complex, and architecture in Bangladesh. He is currently working on a new book, *The Last Hut: Dwelling in the Ascetic Imagination*.

**Dr Ramesh Biswas**, of Malaysian origin, studied in Delhi, Edinburgh and Graz. He runs his architectural practice from Vienna and Kuala Lumpur, with several urban-scale projects in Europe, South America and Asia, including India. He has been a visiting professor in Paris, Buenos Aires, Sydney and Tokyo, and has authored numerous books, among them the critically acclaimed *Metropolis Now! Urban Cultures in Global Cities* (New York, 2000). In 1998 he was selected by 25 heads of government as one of 100 Asia-Europe Young Leaders. His latest book is *Pirate Culture and Urban Life in Delhi* (forthcoming, 2008).

**Prem Chandavarkar** is a director of CnT Architects Pvt. Ltd – a Bangalore-based architectural practice. He is a former executive director of Srishti: School of Art Design & Technology in Bangalore, and is currently a visiting faculty there. He writes and lectures on architecture, art, urbanism, cultural studies and education.

**Sunil Khilnani** is Director of South Asia Studies at The Johns Hopkins School of Advanced International Studies in Washington DC, and author of *The Idea of India* (Penguin, 2003).

**Anupama Kundoo** is an architect whose work, ranging from single houses and housing complexes to public buildings, demonstrates sustainable building techniques that have been the result of years of experimentation and research. She has delivered lectures and conducted workshops in areas related to innovative building construction and building infrastructure, sustainability and issues of globalisation. After graduating from Sir JJ College of Architecture, University of Bombay, she began her architecture practice in Auroville in 1990, with a strong focus on research and experimentation in eco-friendly construction techniques. In 2005 she was awarded the Architect of the Year Award in the group housing category by JK Cement, India. She currently lives in Berlin, where she teaches at the Technical University.

**Reinhold Martin** is Associate Professor of Architecture in the Graduate School of Architecture, Planning, and Preservation at Columbia University, where he directs the PhD programme in architecture, and the Master of Science programme in advanced architectural design. He is a founding co-editor of the journal *Grey Room*, a partner in the firm of Martin/Baxi Architects, and the author of *The Organizational Complex: Architecture, Media, and Corporate Space* (MIT Press, 2003). He is also the co-author, with Kadambari Baxi, of *Entropia* (Black Dog, 2001) and *Multi-National City: Architectural Itineraries* (ACTAR, 2007).

**Anuradha Mathur** is an architect and landscape architect. She is an associate professor at the School of Design, University of Pennsylvania. **Dilip da Cunha** is an architect and city planner. He is faculty at Parsons School of Design, New York, and the University of Pennsylvania. They are the authors of *Mississippi Floods: Designing a Shifting Landscape* (Yale University Press, 2001) and *Deccan Traverses: The Making of Bangalore's Terrain* (Rupa & Co, 2006).

**Adnan Morshed** received his PhD from MIT's History, Theory and Criticism section of Architecture. He is currently an assistant professor at the School of Architecture and Planning, the Catholic University of America, Washington DC, and has been awarded fellowships at the National Gallery of Art, the Smithsonian Institution and Wolfsonian-Florida International University. He has published on the theory and history of Modern architecture and urbanism in the *Journal of the Society of Architectural Historians* and the *Journal of Architectural Education, Thresholds, and Constructs*. His forthcoming book is entitled *The Architecture of Ascension*. A practising architect, he has designed buildings in the US, Lebanon, Malaysia and Bangladesh.

**Michael Sorkin** is the principal of the Michael Sorkin Studio in New York City, a design practice devoted to both practical and theoretical projects at all scales with a special interest in the city and in green architecture. He is also founding president of Terreform, a non-profit organisation dedicated to research and intervention in issues of urban morphology, sustainability, equity and community planning. He has been Professor of Architecture and the Director of the Graduate Urban Design Program at the City College of New York since 2000, and has taught at many institutions worldwide. He is currently a contributing editor at *Architectural Record* and *Metropolis*. Publications include *Wiggle* (Springer-Verlag, 1998), a monograph of the studio's work, and *Against the Wall* (The New Press, 2005).

**Ravi Sundaram** is a fellow at the Centre for the Study of Developing Societies, Delhi, and an initiator of the Sarai programme on media and urban culture (www.sarai.net). His work deals with the intersection of the city and contemporary electronic cultures. He has co-edited a number of publications in the Sarai Readers series including *The Cities of Everyday Life* (2002), and is author of *Pirate Culture and Urban Life in Delhi: After Media* (Routledge, 2007).

# C O N T E N T S

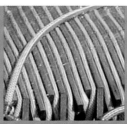

Perched on the edge of a wharf overlooking downtown Boston, Diller Scofidio + Renfro's new Institute of Contemporary Art takes advantage of its strange dramatic site, providing useful, unusually provocative spaces for the various arts it was built to house. While it is not surprising that Diller and Scofidio, who are artists themselves, were able to accommodate the complex programme imaginatively, their new firm's handling of the site in their first freestanding American building is impressive indeed. **Jayne Merkel** explains how the interiors are individualised and energised by the embrace of the harbour in a scheme that minimises the location's drawbacks and turns a visit into an art experience in its own right.

Even the elevator at the ICA is an event in its own right – as big as a room. Its glass walls look out on the harbour and into interior spaces, lining up with their dimensions exactly. A second, regular enclosed elevator accommodates crowds at performances and disabled visitors when the main lift is crowded, and a smooth winding staircase offers more energetic ascent.

When you emerge from a tunnel under the channel that separates the thriving city centre from raw, formerly industrial South Boston, a few mid-rise Postmodern buildings soon give way to a big red-brick federal courthouse by Pei Cobb Freed. Then there is nothing but open space for a while, an ordinary harbourside restaurant and, beyond that, more emptiness, until a rugged concrete Port Authority building with some docks for small ferries appears. A few blocks southeast is Rafael Viñoly's 'World Trade Center' (for conventions), the biggest building in New England (at 157,935 square metres/1.7 million square feet), but even with a sweeping canopied entrance and sleek slanted columns it cannot quite take command. The area around it seems empty, too. No wonder the city offered sites to the ICA, Boston Children's Museum, Fire Museum and a Computer Museum which has already moved away. The neighbourhood is a sea of would-be development sites. Though new hotels, apartments and stores are said to be planned, there is no sign that they are coming any time soon, so the four-storey, 5,760-square-metre (62,000-square-foot) ICA is eerily isolated.

Its strange clamp-like shape, wrapped in a smooth glass-and-steel skin, faces the water with a wide, tall outdoor staircase – a grandstand forming a sort of jagged mouth – sheltered by cantilevered fourth-floor galleries. The building turns its smooth, shiny back on the underdeveloped areas around it. There is an entrance in the rear, but a stretch of the new Boston Harborwalk along the west side makes the entry on the waterfront facade more enticing, as does an outdoor eating area adjacent to an indoor Water Café. Both the north and south entries lead to a generous lobby with a tall, sloped ceiling and views of the Harborwalk; its reception desk offers a glimpse into a colourful little museum store,

Visitors to the Institute of Contemporary Art arrive on the south side, where the main entrance is, but the adventurous wander around to the opposite end where a gigantic staircase facing the water reveals the building's real orientation. A second entrance, also leading to the lobby, runs between the steps and outdoor seating for chef Wolfgang Puck's 85-seat indoor Water Café. Sheltered by galleries cantilevered out from the fourth floor, the big wooden grandstand shelters stepped seating outdoors. Its shape echoes that of the steep-stepped theatre inside on the second and third floors, which is visible from outdoors through its glass walls.

---

**Diller Scofidio + Renfro, Institute of Contemporary Art, Boston, Massachusetts, US, 2006**
All the galleries of the new museum, clad in an opaque glass planking, are located on the top floor where they can be naturally illuminated by a system of adjustable, concealed, filtered skylights and arranged in a continuous run even though their combined 1,672-square metres (18,000 square feet) of space is almost double the building's footprint. A 23-metre (75-foot) cantilever, supported by a steel truss designed by Arup New York, made it possible to group the 4.9-metre (16-foot) high galleries together and shelter the outdoor harbourside staircase at the same time.

tucked under the outdoor staircase. The lobby's dramatic shape is formed by the steeply stepped seating in the theatre upstairs. Interior spaces throughout the building are interlocked to fit compactly into the volume, absorb the harbour views and accommodate the programme in a way that makes each function into an event.

Getting to the upstairs spaces is half the fun. A glass-walled elevator the size of a room – 5.5 metres (18 feet) wide by 2.7 metres (9 feet) deep – looks out on the water and into interior spaces as it carries visitors to the theatre, mediatheque and galleries upstairs. A sexy little staircase wraps around a pole nearby, beckoning, but it is hard to compete with the see-through lift.

Nothing here is quite familiar, but the way the building's clear-glass skin wraps around the theatre in the middle of the structure resembles the wood wrapper that sheathes Diller + Scofidio's 2000 Brasserie restaurant in the Seagram Building, one of their first built works, and their winning, still-unrealised scheme of the next year for the Eyebeam Museum of Art and Technology in New York. (Scofidio designed a number of impressive housing projects before he met and married Diller in the middle of his career.) Most of the work they did together before forming a partnership with Charles Renfro in 2004 was ephemeral – art installations, books, videos and exhibitions (the best known perhaps is the Blur Building, a watery pavilion for Swiss EXPO 02 on Lake Neuchatel). These projects equipped them ideally to design a multimedia art centre like the ICA. The firm's work is adventurous, confident and crisp despite the many curved edges, and curiously functional. Every shape has a purpose.

The overhanging top floor with its very large footprint is able to provide 1,672 square metres (18,000 square feet) of gallery space in one continuous stretch – almost double the footprint of the building would allow – because it projects over the site line. And because the galleries are on top, an expansive, adaptable skylight system can provide filtered

The taut seamless skin of the ICA diagrams the wedge-shaped and rectangular interior spaces that fit together like a Chinese puzzle. Panels of the same size alternate between transparent and translucent glass and opaque metal, blurring the distinction between walls, doors and windows while creating suitable environments for the various activities inside. The curved ribbon-like wrapper contains the theatre, and the wedge hovering over the grandstand houses the mediatheque. Opaque glass walls on the overhanging fourth floor hold light-filled galleries.

**'The Boston Harborwalk borders the north and west edges of the ICA site. This [wooden plank] surface is metaphorically extended into the building as a pliable wrapper that defines its major public spaces. It folds up into a grandstand facing the water, continues through the skin of the building to form a stage, turns up to form the theatre seating, then envelops the theatre space, ultimately slipping out through the skin to produce the ceiling of the exterior public room. Above the wrapper sits the opaque glass "gallery box" that dramatically cantilevers over the Harborwalk towards the water.'**

*Diller Scofidio + Renfro*

natural light from above. All the galleries are on that fourth level, as the director hoped they could be. A long, shallow, glass-walled space on the northern end, called the Founders Gallery, offers a place for gallery goers to relax, take in views of the harbour, and retool. Most cannot resist taking pictures – which end up being pictures of other people taking pictures.

The architects intended to make this space even more unusual by fitting it with lenticular glass that would, as Diller put it, have 'turned the view on and off', slicing it into segments so that each person walking by would see different sections of the harbour, and every walk through the gallery would be a little different from the last. But museum officials could not bear to part with the big wide harbour view that overlooks Logan Airport and the downtown skyline. This is too bad, since one can see the view from numerous other perspectives as one wanders around the place. The lenticular treatment would have created another memorable event.

On the same fourth level as the galleries is a mediatheque where visitors can see the water with no horizon line, because

The tall, narrow 483-square-metre (5,200-square-foot) performing arts theatre stacks the 325 comfortable upholstered seats steeply so that no view is obstructed and a relatively large crowd can be accommodated on a relatively small footprint. The room has a perforated, wave-shaped grey wall on the right side. When theatre goers arrive they usually find black fabric in aluminium frames on the left and behind the stage. But at some point the frames rise to reveal astounding waterfront views – a performance in itself.

The architects, who create videos themselves, have accommodated this art form in a steep, angled, slightly scary space for digital media that is suspended from the underside of the cantilevered fourth floor. This 102-square-metre (1,100-square-foot) mediatheque has individual computer terminals arranged in stepped rows. Views of the harbour here are set at a sharp angle almost straight down, so the horizon line and most of the activities on the water are out of sight.

they look almost straight down through a slanted window that hangs over the outdoor staircase. This strange steep-stepped little theatre-like space, filled with individual computer screens, offers opportunities to view the ICA's collection of videos or learn more about ICA programmes. Although this is a hip way of providing information that usually takes up wall space, it is more valuable for viewing video art, which is rarely efficiently shown in museums. The room has a slightly eerie quality, like that in many artists' videos.

This room, which divides museum goers from one another, resembles the larger 325-seat theatre that brings them together in an equally dramatic way. Although the theatre occupies the second- and third-floor spaces on the west side of the building, its entrance is on the third level. The audience

descend a steep staircase before settling into cushy seats covered with orange upholstery. Its members usually find themselves in a rather dark room with a perforated, wavy grey wall on one side and black fabric set into aluminium frames on the other and in the front. A maze of exposed theatrical lighting hovers overhead. At some point, the frames rise to reveal wall-sized views of the harbour on the north and east. It is beyond spectacular. And it is well used since the ICA has an unusually lively programme of performing arts.

Other spaces on the first and second floors are devoted to the ambitious 119-square-metre (1,280-square-foot) education centre, which contains classrooms, workshops and a digital studio. The building itself does a pretty good job of educating the public by supporting experimental activity, so it is a shame that its trustees decided to begin acquiring a permanent collection when they moved in. Given the price of contemporary art today, and an isolated location five very long blocks from public transport, the money might have been better spent on water taxis from Cambridge, downtown and other lively parts of the city.

Boston is one of the few American cities where you can live (if not too conveniently) without a car. Unfortunately, in these times, planners there have not made transportation a priority in this location. Good transit is more likely to encourage growth than will museums. But given the decision that had been made, the architects, who worked with Perry Dean Rogers Partners of Boston, made the most of an awkward situation. Diller Scofidio + Renfro's subtle handling of a difficult site bodes well for their current work at Lincoln Center and on the High Line in New York, both of which involve urban design more than anything else. ∆+

Text © 2007 John Wiley & Sons Ltd. Images: pp 130, 131(b) © Diller Scofidio + Renfro, photos Nic Lehoux; pp 131(t), 133 © Diller Scofidio + Renfro; p 132 © Diller Scofidio + Renfro, photo Iwan Baan

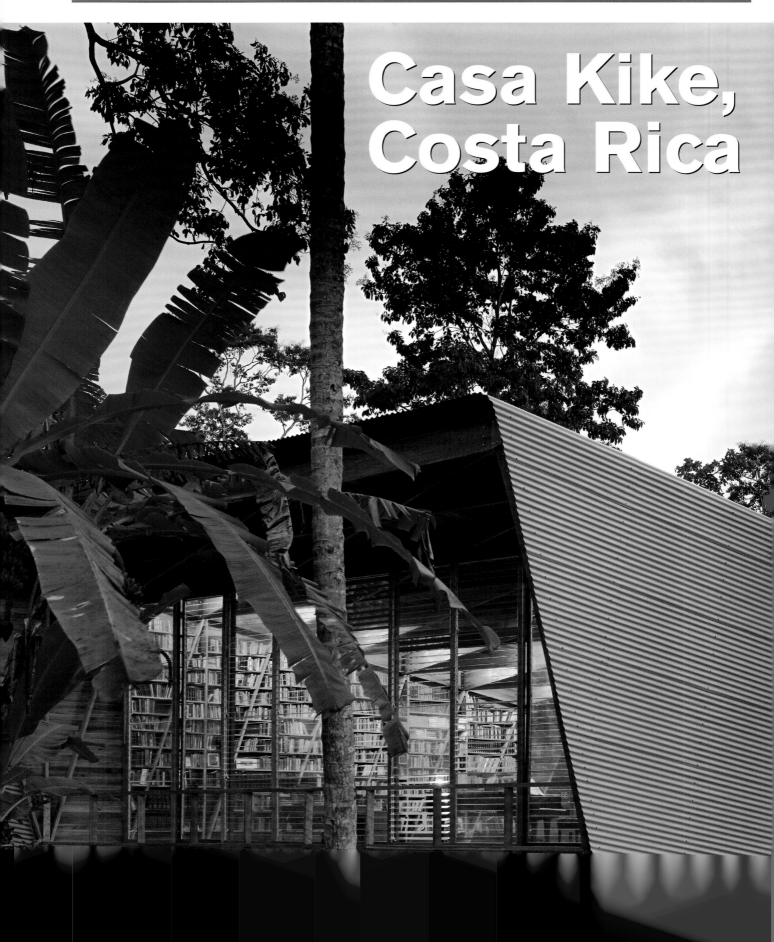

# Casa Kike, Costa Rica

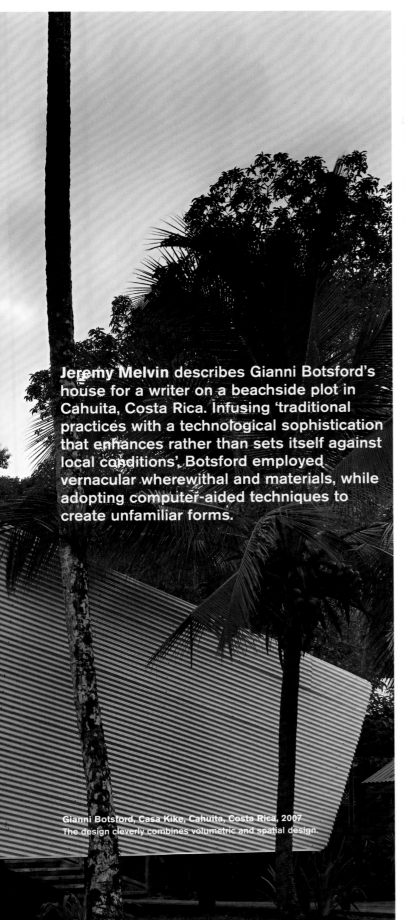

Jeremy Melvin describes Gianni Botsford's house for a writer on a beachside plot in Cahuita, Costa Rica. Infusing 'traditional practices with a technological sophistication that enhances rather than sets itself against local conditions', Botsford employed vernacular wherewithal and materials, while adopting computer-aided techniques to create unfamiliar forms.

Gianni Botsford, Casa Kike, Cahuita, Costa Rica, 2007
The design cleverly combines volumetric and spatial design.

The writer in his jungle: a combination of reason and culture.

Sixteen thousand books and one piano sounds like the writer's house of many a third-year student project, but when set in a tropical rainforest where heat and humidity play havoc with such bourgeois accoutrements, there is no room for complacency. Vernacular traditions may have much to offer the forest's original inhabitants, but they do not write for a living or make a habit of playing Mozart sonatas or reading Saul Bellow. To make a suitable habitat for the hardware of these phenomena of Western culture, every detail, from the choice of materials and construction technique, through cooling and servicing strategies to spatial configuration has to result from a considered decision. And in devising the hardware all sorts of implications for the software – effects, impressions and ideas – come to the surface.

This was the challenge that Gianni Botsford faced when asked to design a house on a tropical paradise – Costa Rica's Caribbean coast. The site is just at the point where the forest gives way to a strip of black-sand beach before the land yields to the ocean. Unlike its neighbours to north and south, Nicaragua and Panama respectively, Costa Rica has taken some elements of its physically paradisiacal setting into its

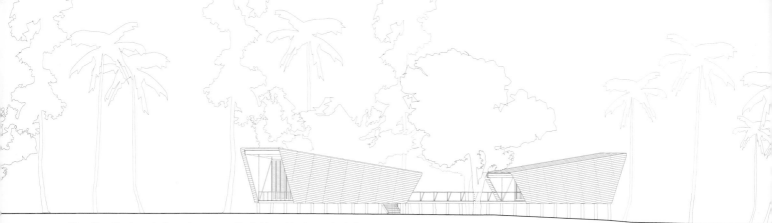

Elevation: the two similar volumes, studio (left) and bedroom (right) face opposite directions.

social structure. Its constitutional principle of not having a standing army inoculates it against the military dictatorships that have arisen across its borders, and social tensions are noticeably less marked.

Its building traditions were similarly naive. There is little genuine local vernacular and most buildings are no more than a few decades old. Simple shacks are the norm in rural areas, while local architects, says Botsford, tend to aspire to air-conditioned, smoked-glass boxes. A small house already on the site meant he could not ignore local ways of building, especially as he had little choice but to use local builders and he also suspected that they would know something about building in the jungle – which he didn't. What he sought to do was to infuse traditional practices with a technological sophistication that enhances rather than sets itself against local conditions as a Modernist box would do.

Botsford is best known in the UK for the Lighthouse, a large, coenobitic house on a backland site in Notting Hill. It is probably the first private new house in London to have its own chapel since the Catholic Emancipation Act, but Botsford's interest in light as an almost sculptural design tool pervades throughout its skilfully articulated volumes.

If his approach to light is sculptural, his chisel is computer-generated fractal patterns. He studied at the AA in London with John Frazer and has spent his 10 or so years in practice further developing the ideas. Computer programs can predict sun paths and show how light will fall on a site. These establish what Le Corbusier might have recognised as *tracé regulateurs*, but based on the fluctuating dynamics of solar patterns rather than static proportions. Volumes start to emerge from these shapes and as they interact with site conditions, programme and construction techniques, they move from abstraction to concrete form.

With its strong, angular shapes the Costa Rica house betrays this approach, though as Botsford explains, here the strategy was more to keep the light out than to entice it in, as at Notting Hill. Its forms bring a dynamism to the location: where the existing house is staid and stable, the new structures – two volumes with a master bedroom facing the jungle and a living room with books and piano opening towards the ocean – are slanted and active. Overall they have a lightness that comes from minimal use of materials, elevation on stilts and careful detailing to prevent clumsy junctions from marring the effect.

The stilts were one of the lessons Botsford took from local builders. There are termites here, and the standard way of dealing with them is to soak trunks of a particular tree in a resistant solution and then place them at 3-metre (9.8-foot)

The interplay between structure and form achieves a dynamic equilibrium.

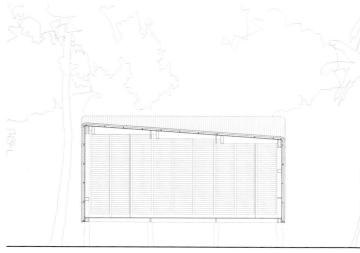

Cross-section through the studio: the angular volumes rest on simple stilts.

With its angular form and metallic finish, the house seems to be an integral part of the jungle.

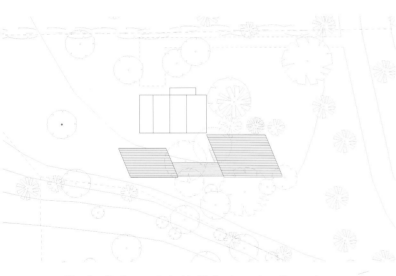

Site plan: the house sits just behind a dune where the sandy beach turns into the rainforest.

centres in a concrete-lined borehole. Botsford's only modification to the traditional practice was to restrict the height of the floor above the ground to 1.2 metres (3.9 feet) so it would not become colonised as an undercroft and the impression of the house floating above the ground would be maintained. Being so close to the sea, there is an almost constant breeze and allowing this to play freely through and around the house helps to keep it habitable.

Above the stilts the structure becomes more innovative. Working with Tall Engineers, Botsford worked out a way of using local materials and skills to create unfamiliar forms. The structure is essentially a timber frame, but in each of the two volumes it wraps around almost like a spiral. Its patterns seem to repeat, but, twisting and expanding or shrinking with

the volume itself, they vary in each case and establish a complex three-dimensional pattern. Within them sit the books, linking the structural concept to the core of the programme. The effect is a remarkably wide clear span where the books dominate side walls, views pan out at either end and timber beams fly overhead.

What quite literally holds this complexity together are the junctions. Understanding how each one would work was a formidable task, requiring computer studies, small folded paper models and drawings. And all had to be interpreted by the six or seven carpenters who had never built anything like it before. Above the frame is a timber lining, and on top of that a reflective insulating layer with an air gap to the corrugated metal cladding. The reflective coat limits how much heat from the sun comes into the room below, while the air gap allows the wind to prevent a temperature build-up. This device, explains Botsford, was worked out in England and is a considerable improvement on local practice. A nearby house built at the same time by the normal means is apparently uninhabitably hot for several hours a day.

Whether lying in the bath and looking into the deeper jungle, or sitting at a writing desk and looking towards the ocean, the interiors are havens for observation. They demonstrate the complexities of human intellect, represented by linear patterns with an origin in mathematics, written knowledge and music, but these cerebral forces do not seem at odds with the bounteous nature around. Indeed as the trees sway in the wind their shadows almost caress the house, as if welcoming it to the locality. It is possible, after all, to improve on nature, just as Botsford has managed to improve on local building traditions. 𝚫+

Text © 2007 John Wiley & Sons Ltd. Images: pp 134-5, 136(bl), 137(t) © Christian Richters; pp 136(t&br), 137(b) © Gianni Botsford Architects

# DSDHA

Less than 10 years old, DSDHA (Deborah Saunt David Hills Architects) has worked its way up the ladder of building types from nurseries, through to schools and now their first university building opened in summer 2007 in Cambridge. **Helen Castle** went to visit the studio in Kennington, south London, and discovered a practice that thrives on the heady mixture that educational buildings offer, combining social engagement with complex client needs.

Visiting DSDHA's studio in Iliffe Yard on the Pullen's Estate is a revelation. Following the practice manager's advice on the phone, I take a black cab to Kennington from Waterloo. The south London taxi driver is not even sure where Iliffe Yard is, but he happily lets me down in Iliffe Street where I find the entrance to the yard's cobbled lane. Despite living in London all my life, this is the first time I have come across the Pullen's Estate, named after its builder James Pullen. The estate consists of some of the last surviving Victorian tenement buildings in the city; the young Charlie Chaplin lived here for several months in 1907. More interestingly, though, the buildings were speculatively developed in the late 19th century as a live–work community for blue-collar workers at a point when employment on the railways was depleting.

Attached to the rear of the housing blocks are three out of four of the original working yards – one of which is Iliffe Yard. Whereas once hansom cab drivers, candlemakers and seamstresses had their workshops here, the yards are now populated by creatives and local businesses, film makers, jewellery designers, costume makers, engineers and architects, as well as cleaners, builders, painters, stonemasons and lute makers. Built of grey stock brick, the workshops are two storeys high and flat-roofed. They have double-floor loading bays edged with blue brick quoins, and the buildings maintain their original window frames and doors and the lanes their cobbles. Inside, they are divided into long thin spaces that are not unlike train carriages connected by doors at each end. DSDHA now has five of these units, having started with only one in 2001 when they relocated from an old record shop in Brixton.

It is one of the only sunny mornings this summer, and windows and doors are flung open in Iliffe Yard. There is a sense of community among the small companies in the yards. They have an open-house event twice a year and there is a familiarity among staff in the various work units who still have to share facilities such as toilets. On DSDHA's doorstep I bump into Claire McDonald, who joined Deborah Saunt and David Hills in 2004 as the firm's third director. She brings me in and introduces me to Deborah Saunt, the practice's frontwoman. In her late 30s, Saunt is elegant, articulate and warm. She walks me through the five work units where 10 or 12 young architects are sitting at their Apple Macs, and talks me through the projects currently on the boards. Though the atmosphere is industrious, there is an easy banter and a sense of camaraderie. There is no doubt that this is a pleasant place to work. It is this sense of enjoyment and aspiration that Saunt desires to engender through the office's own architecture. When in 2001 DSDHA responded to a call for entries from the Department for Education and Skills (DfES) and CABE, they had a single page to get down their conception of what nursery architecture should be. Rather than focusing on simplistic child-centred design, they emphasised the importance of providing a built environment

**Paradise Park Children's Centre and Park Café, Islington, London, 2006**
A Sure Start initiative, this nursery, café and training facility was part of the regeneration of a run-down park in North London. Its key feature is the vertical hydroponic garden covering the front elevation, an innovative response to planning policy that asked for green spaces not to be lost.

that would be formative – for the adult in the child. A nursery space should be uplifting and materially pleasing, providing a child with a positive first experience of architecture and public institutions. Saunt has a strong belief that expectations are embedded in buildings. For her this was formulated by her own childhood experience; when she was seven her parents, with the aid of an architect, transformed their 1930s bungalow in suburban Buckinghamshire into a wonderful 1970s house. Forever building tree houses and camps, she was from then on in no doubt that she wanted to be anything other than an architect.

Despite being a little-known start-up in 2001, DSDHA's pitch to CABE stood out from the competition and resulted in the practice's first most significant commission – the Hoyle Early Years Centre (2003) in Bury, Lancashire. The nursery won them a RIBA Award in 2004 and a British Construction Industry Award in 2005, which recognised their collaborative skills in making buildings representing construction, contractors and client satisfaction as well as design quality; the nursery has also now been adopted as an exemplary project by the Sure Start initiative and CABE.

Since being founded in 1998, DSDHA has worked across a wide range of building types from private houses to large-scale urban planning; they have collaborated with New York office Leroy Street Studio on two houses in the UK (one in Berkshire and another in Kensington) and on a feasibility study for Parliament Square in London with Foster + Partners, as well as on housing for Urban Splash and the urban regeneration scheme The Castleford Project for Channel 4. However, it is on educational projects that one senses that

William Bellamy Children's Centre, Dagenham, Essex, 2006

DSDHA are really in their element, having worked their way up the typological ladder from nurseries, through to schools and now a university building; they are completing the Moller Centre Collaborative Learning Environment for Churchill College, Cambridge, this year. The architects have had repeat work from local boroughs with three nursery buildings from Barking and Dagenham alone. DSDHA seem to thrive under the demands of multi-headed clients. In a nursery centre – the basic model they learnt on – it is necessary not only to design for babies and for mobile toddlers, but also for staff and parents who are often not only collecting children, but also attending the centre for training purposes or as a point of social contact. Saunt extends the conventional definition of the client beyond the owner, or even the user, to reach out to the passer-by who has the exterior experience of their buildings. In their design for Christ's College Secondary School and Pond Meadow Special Needs School in Guildford, Surrey, which is being completed in 2009, DSDHA explicitly asked the council if they could put a public right of way across the land. It was apparent that residents from the adjacent housing estate were having to cut across the secondary school's property in order to avoid a long walk to the primary school. This added another urban level to the project and highlights DSDHA's concern with social engagement.

On leaving Cambridge University in the early 1990s, Saunt's first job was with Sandy Wilson on the British Library. She then went on to work for London architect MJ Long, who was an important mentor. During this time she began early competition entries with David Hills, also a graduate of Cambridge, who had also previously worked with MJ Long. In 1997 she got her first teaching job in Nigel Coates' architecture department at the Royal College of Art. It is evident that Saunt benefited from Coates' emphasis on urban scenario making and narrative. It was, however, Tony Fretton who provided an important revelationary moment for her when she went to see him lecture with Caruso St John. She describes it as a 'door opening'. Fretton understood politics and art, but he also aspired to creating beautiful buildings with wider social ambitions. Saunt had always been convinced that social innovation must be a key generator of architecture, and to hear Fretton talk about people and architecture in the same breath was the discovery of a 'kindred spirit'. It provided her with the realisation that people-centred design need not be a lone path. It was the same feeling for Saunt as reading Venturi and Scott Brown in college when she studied in America, or John Evelyn's 17th-century writing on architecture at Cambridge. She felt as if she had found her place. This confidence was perhaps boosted by the chance to run a Diploma Studio at Cambridge with David Hills, where the two began to formulate the bones of their shared architecture direction to set up DSDHA. It was further consolidated by a two-year period working in Fretton's

## William Bellamy Children's Centre, Dagenham, Essex, 2006

This new children's centre at William Bellamy Infant School is situated near the civic centre of Dagenham. It provides crèche facilities for the under-fives and daycare for children attending the school, as well as outdoor space for play. The aluminium panels of the exterior are an allusion to Dagenham's recent past as one of the UK's main car-producing areas. The tower makes it a point of focus in a monotonous urbanscape of postwar civic buildings and housing.

## Christ's College Secondary School and Pond Meadow Special Needs School, Guildford, Surrey, due for completion 2009

The secondary school is part of a new flagship educational campus in Guildford, which also includes Pond Meadow Special Needs School. The brief for this Church of England school, which promotes religious education and pastoral care, emphasised the need for a centralised space to encourage the inclusive spirit of the school community, and a dedicated space for worship. DSDHA symbolically represent this idea in the notion of 'One House' with a single front door, welcoming all pupils, staff and visitors. This provides a portal through which the four individual schoolhouses and facilities are accessed. Christ's College will be the first school in the UK to utilise an integrated heat-recovery system that transfers the body heat from the users into energy for the building's heating and ventilation.

office on a series of art gallery projects and exhibitions. Saunt likens the experience to a 'masterclass'.

The office is now nine years old and DSDHA have learnt as much from research and theory as through their built work. It is the combination of research and practice that Saunt believes has singled them out from their contemporaries:

'We have assiduously cultivated and evolved a position and approach that is fundamentally derived from a research base; of looking at the interstices of where architecture and society collide, or where social and technical innovation can create a new urban landscape and architecture can be formed. All of our projects with students focus on city-scale analysis (landscape/topography, historic layers, local culture, public consultation, movement and view analysis and socioeconomic evaluation) as well as the micro – the material responses, the formal communication, the landscape of the interior in juxtaposition with the landscape of the city, a sense of tension at every scale. It is through our research that we managed to break into urban design as well as making buildings – simply by carrying out urban research with our students and disseminating the results so that we were taken seriously at this scale.

'David and I have always taught – at the RCA, Cambridge and AA – now David will be teaching again at Cambridge, and Harry Gugger at Herzog & de Meuron has asked if I can teach in Switzerland next year. So it has been a happy coincidence of combining research to inform and lead the work in practice. We like to make, but we also theorise a great deal, and ask if a solution is being derived in a "DSDHA" way; that is, not on a whim, but through proper parametric evaluation.'

Saunt has a strong belief in the iterative process, evolving and getting better through the construction of projects. This stands in contrast to the practices who are a decade or so older and developed almost exclusively through paper architecture and theoretical research; the most conspicuous and prominent international examples being the formalism of Zaha Hadid or Daniel Libeskind. Much of DSDHA's research has centred on experimentation of materials, whether it is the installation of dry-stone walls in the Hoyle Early Years Centre, vertical gardens at Paradise Park Children's Centre, or the use of aluminium cladding in the William Bellamy Children's Centre in Dagenham. DSDHA try never to use the same material twice. There is a sense that the office is approaching a new juncture. Saunt is eager to take it to a new level: 'Now we've built some buildings, it is about developing the physical and intellectual duration of projects.'

Rather than seeking duration through an identifiable vocabulary of elements, insisting like some signature architects on repetition of elements ad infinitum so that the same door or window details, for instance, are rolled out across every project, Saunt is keen to create a rhetorical

## John Perry Children's Centre, Dagenham, Essex, 2004/2006

This competition-winning scheme for the London Borough of Barking and Dagenham provided a master plan for a purpose-built, 26-place nursery, along with a 50-place daycare facility that was built two years later. It is set within a socially challenged area, and one of DSDHA's ambitions was to connect the children with nature and the world beyond, rather than reinforcing the domestic realm – creating public buildings for children. Whereas the polycarbonate walls are translucent and define the interior as studio space, the cantilevered canopy and reacting doors encourage children to wander outside to play.

# Moller Centre Collaborative Learning Environment, Churchill College, Cambridge, 2007

DSDHA won this project on merit of their proposed planning of the site, which separated the new music recital rooms and the conference areas from the college's back-of-house facilities. The exterior has a sleek glass elevation that reflects the exceptional landscaping of Churchill College, filtering the views passers-by have of the interior. Inside, the timber lining softens the sharp geometry of the structure and complements the wooded landscape outside.

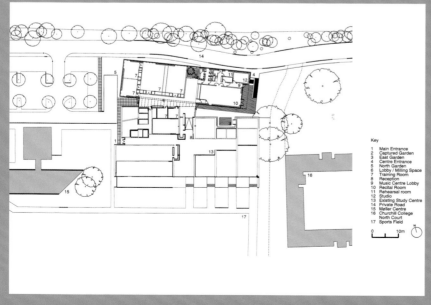

Key

1 Main Entrance
2 Captured Garden
3 East Garden
4 Centre Entrance
5 North Garden
6 Lobby / Milling Space
7 Training Room
8 Reception
9 Music Centre Lobby
10 Recital Room
11 Rehearsal room
12 Studio
13 Existing Study Centre
14 Private Road
15 Moller Centre
16 Churchill College
   North Court
17 Sports Field

0        10m

## Hoyle Early Years Centre, Bury, Lancashire, 2003

Commended by the RIBA and its users alike, in 2004 the RIBA Awards described it as a building that 'does not shout about its architectural ambitions but is an exemplary building that works for the staff and children, all of whom are much less stressed than before. One might say that this is working towards a new vernacular';[1] while its headmistress values it for being 'super – it is light and airy – the total opposite of the previous building'.[2] The initial intention was to alter and extend an original 1970s nursery building that was situated next to a local authority housing estate in a deprived area of Bury that runs alongside the M66. It proved cheaper though to almost completely demolish it, with only some of its walls and materials being retained in the new building. The main elevation to the street is clad with dry-stone walling, which Saunt describes as 'making evident' and 'cherishing the natural qualities of the site'. Inside, the building is light and airy with white walls, high ceilings and clerestory windows.

language that is purposeful. She traces this back to the enormous influence of Rem Koolhaas, Robert Venturi and Denise Scott Brown on her generation, with the notion of architecture as communication or a sign, and cites as an example of this in DSDHA's own work the big cantilevered canopy above the door of the John Perry Children's Centre in Dagenham. It provides a big sheltering sign for the door, and without columns it is rhetorical and provocative, questioning the conventions of built structure.

Recently asked by Italian architects in Milan at the launch of the *AD* issue on Italy about the younger generation of British architects, I emphasised the way that architects under 40 have been influenced by the experience of building. DSDHA epitomise this definition of a successful London practice. They have effectively grown up under the premiership of Tony Blair. They have been shaped by the opportunities to build in the public sector, particularly educational buildings, whereas the generation of the 1980s and early 1990s were often shaped by the very paucity of available commissions, which led them to the visionary. This is in a sense a very privileged position to be in. Saunt is very positive about her clients and the opportunities that they have afforded. Educational buildings are not, however, without their difficulties. It is not only the complex nature of the briefs and the clients, but also the tight budgets they are often forced to adhere to in the public sector. There is no doubt that this can be detrimental to an architect's social ambitions for a building in a deprived area. In Ellis Woodman's review of DSDHA's Emmaus Primary School in a run-down area of Sheffield in the *Architect's Journal* (11 May 2007), Woodman is candid about the fact that despite the 'scheme being robust enough' to survive chops in budget, 'there are moments where the belt-tightening leaves the building a mite too pinched for comfort'. An architect might be able to advise his or her client, but it is ultimately the client's choice as to how and where they will spend their money, especially when cuts are imposed from elsewhere.

Until now the practice has been almost entirely UK based, but there is every indication that Saunt will use her clarity of vision to take the office to an international level; DSDHA has just started work on an impressive sustainable resort in the Caribbean and has recently won a competition for a new urban quarter in Accra with Allford Hall Monaghan Morris. The day following my interview with Deborah Saunt I meet with the dean of an architecture school in the US who has also independently found his way to DSDHA's offices. At the annual architecture lecture at the Royal Academy this year, Liz Diller of Diller Scofidio + Renfro proclaimed that she was not a visionary, but interested in engaging in contemporary culture. This tends to suggest that DSDHA's desire 'to engage' rather than to make stylistic or formal statements could also be at the spearhead of a greater international shift. *AD*+

Helen Castle is Editor of *Architectural Design* and Executive Commissioning Editor of the John Wiley & Sons UK architecture list.

Notes
1. www.architecture.com/go/Architecture/Also/Awards_3186.html?q=Hoyle
2. www.cabe.org.uk/default.aspx?contentitemid=343&field=sectionsearchterm&term=Hoyle&type=1

Text © 2007 John Wiley & Sons Ltd. Images: pp 138, 140(t), 141, 142 © Hélène Binet; p 139 © Edmund Sumner/VIEW; p 140(b) © DSDHA; p 143 © Martine Hamilton Knight

# Good-Natured Stuff

**Neil Spiller** ruminates on nature and what 'the odd naughty leaf' has contributed to art and architecture over the years – culminating in evolutionary design and parametrical modelling today. He flags up the work of two of the most 'talented young bucks' in the field – Dennis Dollens and Cloud 9. But how realistic is it for us to really expect biomimicry to influence how and what we build?

Architects have been intent on imitating nature ever since our profession reared its ugly head in dark, dank, bat-dropping infested caves. We decorated these caves with what we saw outside (cattle, deer, tigers) and what we saw inside ourselves once we chewed on the odd naughty leaf (shamanistic figures with wild heads). The Egyptians had lotus columns and the like, the Romans the acanthus and so on until the 1960s with David Greene's Logplug, through the 1990s with John Frazer's Evolutionary Architecture and on to the hip young things of today with their parametric modelling, their evolutionary design software and gorgeously shiny green credentials. Zoomorphic design is in vogue. Two of the talented young bucks of our new age are Dennis Dollens and Cloud 9. Dollens describes his work in relation to the biomimetic which

has, over the last 10 years, become important in the descriptive process of our practice; biomimetics

illuminates only one aspect of the design process. In looking to nature, specifically to botany, as a source for form, structure, spatial organisation, material development, etc, biomimetics plays a primary and indispensable role. Yet other parallel concerns enter the design process, including the attempt to fuse biologically inspired design with computational evolution, new materials (bio-synthetics), and industrial fabrication along with more intangible, but nevertheless indispensable influences from the history of science and philosophy.

Cloud 9's (principal Enric Ruiz Geli) work consists of aviaries developed as synthetic trees and villas that have an aesthetic of biological cell structures utilising mitochondrial shapes and nucleic cores, for example.

How does any of this reconcile itself with the global, viral and virulent capitalist imperative, I hear you ask. An

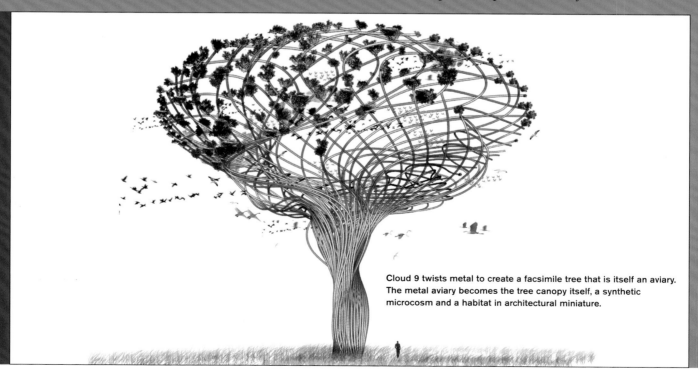

Cloud 9 twists metal to create a facsimile tree that is itself an aviary. The metal aviary becomes the tree canopy itself, a synthetic microcosm and a habitat in architectural miniature.

A-Existing pine tree "pi de bofarull" 25 m high x 40 m diameter  B- Sculpted trees using 3dmax software  C- Fifteen branches, handmade drawings by asian artist  D- Map of links of the 3D model, 22 points  E- Path 3D model, 10 m long  F- Model of the polygons, different diameters from 80cm to 50cm  G- Development of 63 polygons using Xemzf software  H- Rombord pattern calculated from the closing forces applied in autoCAD  80% transparency  I- Sustainability plan for the size of a 2x1 m stainless steel plate, by the laser cutter software system  J- Plan of the laser cutter path  K- Laser cutter ready for stainless steel, 4 mm thickness  L- Laser in use  M- Cutting process, a 4m long branch = 8 hours  N- Blending process, 30 J + 0- Duodecahedric polygon  P-S- Prototype images  T- 3D modelling of the 4 m long branch prototype  U- Artificial PVC mesh, external skin of the HP capsule  V- Natural coconut fabric mesh, interior skin of the HP capsule  W- Hydroponic (HP) cultivation capsule  X- Relationship between the Aviary mesh prototype and a few birds.

Dennis Dollens is aware that his architectural world is reminiscent of Marvel's comic-book heroes. This is an architecture for the contemporary designerly Fantastic Four to inhabit. Buildings sprout branches and shield themselves and power themselves with architectural leaves.

imperative that seeks to ubiquitise devalued skilled labour, economic building funding modelling, capital repayment models, building payback periods and simple economic form? How does it successfully negotiate the convivial orthogonal conspiracy of developers, politicians and their lapdog architects? Well, alas it does not. Very little of this type of work is being built, not because it is silly, but because the market's internal validation system and its consequent fear of originality seeks to turn all it encompasses into conformity. Any work of this type that is currently being built is normally for rich domestic clients, and these are few and far between.

So why do architects and architectural students entertain these fantasies of formal contortion. The answer is that 'Architecture' is a much bigger subject than 'Building'. It is only by formal, theoretical and technical experiment that we may stand a chance of mitigating the disasters that so-called rational and pragmatic architects have enabled and facilitated for much of the 20th century.

But let us not rush to fully embrace a biological imperative that is also fraught with its own ethical problems: the moment plain old-fashioned architectural mimicry becomes, as I am sure technology will lead us to, actual architectural biology. My worry is a simple one, in a world where it can take decades to come to the simple realisation that we are destroying our planet, let alone do anything about it of any real significance; in a world where there have been hundreds of wars, conflicts, genocides (or whatever the politicians of the day call them) since the end of the Second World War; and where life and our bodies are perhaps the world's cheapest commodity. What might happen if we start to build out of flesh? If we can master stem cells, if we can understand autopoiesis and we can build fleshed evolutionary systems, what then?

Fields of eyes and walls of arms – Bosch might not have been just a religious nutter after all. Could this ever be a good thing? From all the evidence I see around me, capital will decide, not you or me! *Δ+*

Neil Spiller is Professor of Architecture and Digital Theory and Vice Dean at the Bartlett School of Architecture, University College London.

Text © 2007 John Wiley & Sons Ltd. Images: pp 144 & 145(r) © Enric Ruiz-Geli © Cloud 9; p 145(l) © Dennis Dollens

# On Green Design (Part 2)
# The Basic Premises for Green Design

In the second part of his green design series, **Ken Yeang** highlights how a prospective site can provide the essential springboard for eco-masterplanning. A full survey of the site and its sensitive development allows the built environment not only to be designed analogously with existing ecological systems, but also to reach out beyond the immediate footprint and to have a restorative effect on the surrounding area.

1. Many architects rush to place buildings upon the site without considering the site's ecological features. Design must respect the natural features of the locality. All building takes place within an ecosystem or on part of nature, and it is vitally important to discern what is existent in the ecology of the locality before imposing any built form or roads or infrastructure or any human activity upon it. This is the fundamental basis for eco-masterplanning.

2. Ecosystems in a biosphere are definable units containing both biotic and abiotic constituents acting together as a whole. From this concept, our businesses and built environment should be designed analogously to the ecosystem's physical content, composition and processes. For instance, besides regarding our architecture as just art objects or as serviced enclosures, we should regard it as artefacts that need to be operationally and eventually integrated with nature.

3. As is self-evident, the material composition of our built environment is almost entirely inorganic, whereas ecosystems contain a complement of both biotic and abiotic constituents, or of inorganic and organic components.

Our myriad construction, manufacturing and other activities are, in effect, making the biosphere more and more inorganic, artificial and increasingly biologically simplified. To continue without balancing the biotic content means simply adding to the biosphere's artificiality, thereby making it more and more inorganic. Exacerbating this are other environmentally destructive acts such as deforestation and pollution. This results in the biological simplification of the biosphere and the reduction of its complexity and diversity.

We must first reverse this trend and start by balancing our built environment with greater levels of biomass, ameliorating biodiversity and ecological connectivity in built forms and complementing their inorganic content with appropriate biomass.

4. Any masterplanning should seek to improve the ecological linkages between our designs and our business processes with the surrounding landscape, both horizontally and vertically. Achieving these linkages ensures a wider level of species connectivity, interaction, mobility and sharing of resources across boundaries. Such real improvements in connectivity enhance biodiversity and further increase habitat resilience and species survival.

**TR Hamzah & Yeang Sdn Bhd (sister company to Llewellyn Davies Yeang), Mewah Oils Headquarters, Kuala Lumpur, Malaysia, 2003**
The project is an experiment to incorporate and integrate biomass inside a building to enhance its biodiversity in a continuous nexus of vegetation that starts from the ground and rises *en escalier* up to the uppermost level of the building.

**Biomass that climbs upwards to the rooftop garden.**

Providing landscaped ecological bridges, tunnels and linkages in regional planning is crucial in making urban patterns more biologically viable.

Besides improved horizontal connectivity, vertical connectivity within the built form is also necessary since most buildings are not single but multistorey. Design must extend ecological linkages upwards within the built form to its roofscapes.

5. More than enhancing ecological linkages, we must biologically integrate the inorganic aspects and processes of our built environment with the landscape so that they mutually become ecosystemic (See (4) above). We must create 'human-made ecosystems' compatible with the ecosystems in nature. By doing so, we enhance the ability of human-made ecosystems to sustain life in the biosphere.

6. Ecodesign is also about conserving the ecology of the site. Any activity from our design or our business must take place with the objective of physically integrating seamlessly and benignly with the ecosystems.

How do we go about looking at the ecological properties of the locality's ecosystem before imposing our human activity upon it? Every site has its own unique ecology with a limiting capacity to withstand stresses imposed upon it, which if stressed beyond this capacity becomes irrevocably damaged. Consequences can range from minimal localised impact (such as the clearing of a small land area for access), to the total devastation of the entire land area (such as the

clearing of all trees and vegetation, levelling the topography, diversion of existing waterways, etc).

7. To identify all aspects of this carrying capacity, we need to carry out an analysis of the site's ecology.

We must ascertain its ecosystem's structure and energy flow, its species diversity and other ecological properties. Then we must identify which parts of the site (if any) have different types of structures and activities, and which parts are particularly sensitive. Finally, we must consider the likely impacts of the intended construction and use.

8. This is, of course, a major undertaking. It needs to be done diurnally over the year and in some instances over years. To reduce this lengthy effort, landscape architects developed the 'layer-cake' method, or a sieve-mapping technique of landscape mapping. This enables the designer to map the landscape as a series of layers in a simplified way to study its ecology.

As we map the layers, we overlay them, assign points, evaluate the interactions in relation to our proposed land use and patterns of use, and produce the composite map or guide our planning (for example, the disposition of the access roads, water management, drainage patterns and shaping of built form(s), etc).

We must be aware that the sieve-mapping method generally treats the site's ecosystem statically and may ignore the dynamic forces taking place between the layers and within an ecosystem. Between each of these layers are complex interactions. Thus analysing an ecosystem requires more than mapping. We must examine the interlayer relationships.

9. These techniques were developed over 20 years ago, but what we need to do now is to extend them to any built forms that are to be located within the site. We need to ensure ecological nexus within the site. The site must not be chopped or fragmented into disparate parcels separated by roads and impervious surfaces. The master plan after it has been laid out with roads and so on must remain holistically interconnected by ecological connectors.

10. The ecological master plan must also create linkages with ecosystems outside the design-site area, as ecological corridors or fingers. These can be used to rehabilitate or restore devastated ecosystems or ecosystems fragmented or divided by inconsiderate human developments. ⌂+

Kenneth Yeang is a director of Llewellyn Davies Yeang in London and TR Hamzah & Yeang in Kuala Lumpur, Malaysia. He is the author of many articles and books on ecodesign, including *Ecodesign: A Manual for Ecological Design* (Wiley-Academy, 2006).

Text © 2007 John Wiley & Sons Ltd. Images © TR Hamzah & Yeang Sdn Bhd

# McLean's Nuggets

## Checking Out

Recently covered in the architectural press was the completion of Toyo Ito's wavy-roofed concrete shell of Kakamigahara Crematorium in Japan – a rare piece of funerary architecture worth an honourable mention. It is unfortunately the case (certainly in the UK) that the design of these 'human termini' are often moribund modal-change places, with none of the slick-serviced facility of the self-storage environment or the well-composed phenomenology of the metaphysical. It is difficult to understand why these programmatic gems have failed to capture the imagination of such an opportunistic architectural profession. Countless rehearsal of such projects in architectural schools has so far failed to materialise in what still remains a rather neglected branch of municipal waste management. So what great contemporary entropic realms can we look to? There is, of course, Aldo Rossi's Rationalist Palais de Death at San Cataldo, Modena, Italy, of 1971, or *Gonzo* journalist Hunter S Thompson's more inflammatory departure, his ashes fired out of a 50-metre (150-foot) high cannon at his Woody Creek estate in Aspen. (His wife Anita commenting that, 'He loved explosions.') This was certainly more salubrious than Louis Kahn's low-budget exit on the washroom floor of New York's Penn Station.

Professor Hilary J Grainger, the sage of UK crematorium design, has stated that crematoria have 'become the invisible buildings of the 20th century ... because no-one wants to talk about the architecture of death'. Widely published in the field, Professor Grainger's books include *'Distressingly Banal': The Architecture of Early British Crematoria*[1] and *Death Redesigned*,[2] which surveys all 251 crematoria in the UK. If all this sounds rather ordinary, then why not join the select list of an estimated 300 'Celestial Burials' (including *Star Trek* creator Gene Roddenberry) where Space Services Inc[3] of Houston, Texas, will put a gram of your ashes into Low-Earth Orbit for a very reasonable $1,295 to circle the earth for between 10 and 240 years depending on the altitude, or was that attitude? For all you carbon-footprint junkies, though, the question is do you choose a one-off carbon emission into the atmosphere (a cremation requires an energy consumption estimated at 300 kWh)[4] plus residual mercury pollution (contained within amalgam tooth fillings), or the long- to medium-term rental of a plot of scarce ground from your local authority for biodegrading purposes?

The Reintegration, part of Andrew Garton's ambitious project To Be Transferred, a 1-kilometre (0.6-mile) long excavated fissure where the forgotten remains of San Jose Cemetery are released and dissolved into the water off the spectacular peninsula of Cadiz.

## Smells Good

According to Mintel, the consumer, media and market research group, the UK deodorant market is currently worth £460 million per annum.[5] Unilever, the Anglo-Dutch multinational, has a 55.4 per cent share of the market, which it hopes to increase with its new Active Response products that are claimed to combat 'emotional sweating' triggered by excitement or stress. However, smell, odour and fragrance remain a largely neglected branch of the architect's palette. Usman Haque, with Josephine Pletts and Dr L Turin, explored the spatial design potential of fragrance in the 2002 project Scents of Space[6] at UCL. Working with building services consultants Max Fordham, they created a three-dimensional stratified environment within which fragrance and odour could be deployed utilising Haque's ongoing (and increasingly sophisticated) research into the social and technological nature of 'interactive' or 'responsive' environments.

Smell-O-Vision, created by Swiss osmologist Hans Laube, was designed to release 30 different smells during the 1960 film *Scent of Mystery*. In 1982 film director John Walters launched his own low-budget scratch-and-sniff 'Odorama' to coincide with the release of his cult film *Polyester*.

## Unplanned

In May 2007, 'All Planned Out' coincided with the 60th anniversary of the Town and Country Planning Act. Organised by Ian Abley's Audacity group, this planning fest hosted at the Building Centre in London was provocative, stimulating and more exciting than a two-day planning conference should possibly be. The underlying theme of the event was largely sub-urban, with much talk about the renewed promise of the Garden City. The example of Hampstead Garden Suburb was cited, but with a pointed reminder from Jules Lubbock (University of Essex) that not so much as a garden shed can be erected with the draconian aesthetic controls in place; add to that Ebenezer Howard's built-in sobriety of the Pub-less suburbs and this model seems less fun. The first day was introduced by Kate Moorcock-Abley with some mind-blowing graphics illustrating the physical impossibility of building anything in the UK, an animated annotation sequentially showing conservation areas, national parks, green belt, stewardship and a host of other land-use controls. James Stephens of English Heritage was refreshingly critical of the conservation-area boom. There are now 9,500 conservation areas as opposed to the 100 in 1970. He was not certain that these measures were to conserve areas of exceptional architectural or social merit, but a form of house-price protectionism. Other highlights of the first day included Michael Savage (Royal Bank of Scotland) who discussed the quality of homes – not just having one, but a good one – and tenants' rights; and Yolande Barnes (Savills Research) on land scarcity and how escalating land value makes the cost of building a less significant component of 'house prices'.

The event's first day closed with a vintage two-hour address by Will Alsop (minimal notes, no images) who invoked the usefulness of art, the problems with democracy (dictators get things done) and why Richard Rogers' Urban Renaissance densification argument is not so bad. At least, Alsop said, when you get outside of your minimal living city dwelling you might find yourself somewhere and within some reasonable proximity of physical and social servicing (shops, schools, social gathering places and so on). During the second day I was lucky enough to chair a session with James Woudhuysen, Michael Trudgeon, Owen Hatherley and Andrew Rabeneck. Woudhuysen launched the group with an excellent and coruscating attack on current UK building culture and practice in all its 'Tudor-bethan excess', describing the UK construction industry (and yes this includes architects) as 'world leaders in backwardness'. He asked why we do not utilise manufactured homes in addition to the one-off, and forget about the religion of place-making and behaviour control and sort out infrastructure and quality of jobs. Trudgeon (Crown Productions) discussed the popular pattern houses of the 18th century and California's Case Study project of the 1950s; his industrial design approach to architecture would utilise a USB-type standardisation of arterial building services systems allowing for mass customisation. Hatherly (Birkbeck) asked what we can learn from the Congres International d'Architecture Moderne (CIAM) and how the large Soviet housing projects of the 1920s were designed around the 'Social Condenser' with artists and architects. Rabeneck (Imperial College) argued that the desire to be modern may damn the past, and that the romance of the manufacturing

industry may be overstated. It is, he said, our job to write the specification, the programme of what to build, not just how to build it.

This event did not have answers: Thomas Sieverts (City Planner, Cologne) asked for new models for the countryside and revisited the (maybe misplaced) optimism that he experienced in post-Second World War New-Town Britain. James Heartfield[7] (Audacity) asked for 5 million new homes in the next 10 years, but 5 million of what and where? The volume UK house builders talk a good game (represented here by John Stewart of the House Builders Federation) while producing (albeit incrementally more efficiently) suburban box houses of narcoleptic mediocrity. ∆+

'McLean's Nuggets' is an ongoing technical series inspired by Will McLean and Samantha Hardingham's enthusiasm for back issues of AD, as explicitly explored in Hardingham's AD issue The 1970s is Here and Now (March/April 2005).

Will McLean is joint coordinator of technical studies (with Peter Silver) in the Department of Architecture at the University of Westminster.

Notes
1. Dr Hilary Grainger, 'Distressingly Banal': The Architecture of Early British Crematoria, Pharos International (UK), 2000.
2. Dr Hilary Grainger, Death Redesigned: British Crematoria – History, Architecture and Landscape, Spire Books Ltd (UK), 2006.
3. www.memorialspaceflights.com/services_orbital.asp
4. www.bbc.co.uk/blogs/newsnight/2007/04/ill_compost_your_corpse_1.html
5. Mintel, Consumer Goods Europe, March 2007, No 532.
6. www.haque.co.uk/
7. James Heartfield, Let's Build!, Audacity (London), 2006.

Text © 2007 John Wiley & Sons Ltd. Images: p 148(l) © Andrew Garton; p 148(r) © From Wired Blog Network (blog.wired.com/.../2006/12/a_brief_history.html), A Brief History of Smell-O-Vision, by John Brownlee, 7 December 2006

# Sensible Objects for Digital Environments

Based in Milan, dotdotdot is poised to optimise on a client base of multinational brands, finance and real estate that takes part in the city's international shows and fairs. **Valentina Croci** explains how this young Italian practice has set out to develop its interactive installations with a 'participative dynamic' that enables clients to effectively communicate their message through the immediate and exclusive involvement of the visitor.

dotdotdot, Interactive surface for Seaway, 'Sali in cortile', Porta Venezia, Milan, 2007
In this interactive installation for Seaway, an interactive surface projected on to the floor is animated by the passage of visitors. Movement is captured by a video camera connected to a computer and a video projector, which re-presents the image with just a short delay. The surface thus becomes like a liquid that shifts under the changing weight.

**dotdotdot, Interactive table for Seaway, 'Sali in cortile', Porta Venezia, Milan, 2006**
This interactive table for Seaway (a Milan-based sailing school that also issues licences for sailing, and offers general services for sports craft and pleasure boating) uses movement sensors for touch-less interaction. The movement of the visitor above the table modifies an electromagnetic field, activating the content of the installation. A fundamental part of this installation is the design of the interface and the direction of access to information.

The design of temporary, interactive installations is one of the more significant harbingers of experimentation in the field of design. The recent development of digital technologies has allowed for a significant reduction in production costs, making this type of installation accessible to a wider clientele. All the same, the field of interactive digital installations is still largely unexplored and difficult to define. They are often seen as one-off artistic installations, and we do not yet fully understand their potential serial applications, such as in the world of retail, the design of urban spaces or private and public signage.

Only in the last five years have a few Italian architectural offices begun to investigate this particular field of design. Milan appears to be the most suitable context given the ease of contact with local and multinational companies and the numerous fairs – not only those of design and fashion, but also, for example, lighting design and real estate. One office that stands out above the crowd is dotdotdot, which was formed in 2004 and has four partners all in their early 30s (architects Laura Dellamotta and Giovanni Gardi, industrial designer Fabrizio Pignoloni and philosopher Alessandro Masserdotti). The multidisciplinary composition of the office is

no accident: their different backgrounds allow them to combine a humanist approach to the behaviour of people in a given environment with more pragmatic issues resolved through design.

As the members of dotdotdot explain, the fundamental problem related to the design of interactive digital installations is not so much the application of technologies as the definition of what the users experience. The technologies are simply the instrument for creating a level of interactive perception and personalising the needs of the client. dotdotdot has completed installations for Rolex, BMW, Deutsche Bank, Seaway, the Milan Chamber of Commerce and the Associazione Zona Tortona. The message being communicated by its clients is presented through the immediate and exclusive involvement of the visitor: the interactive environments created by the installation are capable of playfully reacting to the specific movements of each single user, generating unexpected effects. It is this participative dynamic that represents the added value of these installations. Interaction is thus tied to the actions of the user and the relations between the body and the environment.

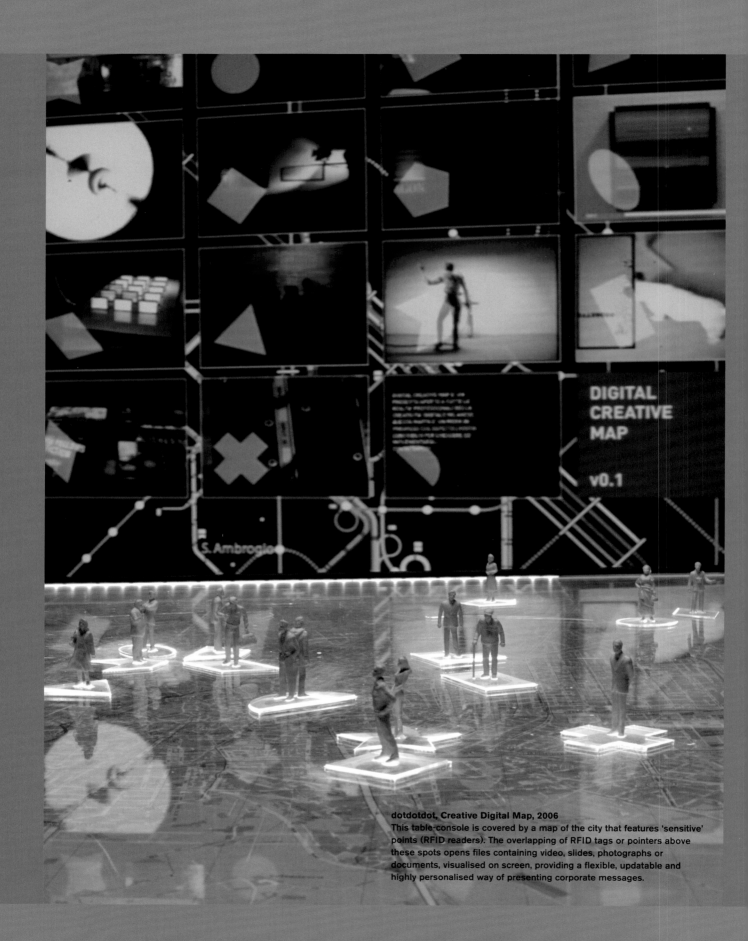

DIGITAL
CREATIVE
MAP

v0.1

S. Ambrogio

**dotdotdot, Creative Digital Map, 2006**
This table-console is covered by a map of the city that features 'sensitive'
points (RFID readers). The overlapping of RFID tags or pointers above
these spots opens files containing video, slides, photographs or
documents, visualised on screen, providing a flexible, updatable and
highly personalised way of presenting corporate messages.

**dotdotdot, Interactive mirror for BMW, Milan Furniture Fair, 2007**
The interactive mirror is run by a video camera hidden behind the glass. Connected to a computer that uses video tracking software, it maps the actions of the faces reflected in the mirror's surface. The system reacts to variation, in the gestures of the users, displaying written messages above their heads like bubble captions in comic strips. The content of the messages can be predefined or text messages from mobile phones can be used.

Primarily because they conceal the communication of a commercial message, these installations must be proposed to a differentiated audience, with no need for technical training or a special understanding of information technologies. dotdotdot have developed RFID (radio frequency identification) technologies related to the Arduino platform – used to detect and convert frequencies – creating objects and physical spaces in which this technology is hardly visible. For example, the Creative Digital Map table-console allows users to access content by simply moving and repositioning a pointer on the table. This simple gesture allows for the on-screen visualisation of multiple and overlapping sources of information. Thus the work of the designer is not only that of designing the interface, but also the definition of the sequences of access to the content and the 'direction' of the interaction. The versatility of RFID technology allows for the construction of interactive supports using any type of surface

such as, for example, vertical sheets of glass or plexiglas or large walls. In this case it is possible to create immersive environments similar to theatre sets, completely modifying the morphology of space and the sensorial perception that users have of it, while maintaining the architectural geometry. This means that, with respect to temporary installations that require a significant use of solid materials, the interactive surfaces create space without matter, that are lightweight, flexible and, above all, sustainable. In this way architecture and installation become a single object.

dotdotdot also designs interactive paving surfaces that change their configuration in response to the passage of visitors – particularly suited for 'pass-thru' installations. The paving can be animated with audio and visual effects, creating significant potential for the communication of company brands. Furthermore, as with the interactive mirror for BMW, the visual sequences, the result of the mapping of the user's movements, can be overlapped in real time from mobile phone text messages: 'a thought for each visitor, and a face for each thought'. This method of interaction amplifies the component of active participation, the primary objective of this type of installation.

The company has also just completed the prototype for an interactive display window for the Associazione Zona Tortona. The installation is to be used for the promotion of *Fuori Salone* (off-site) events during the Milan Furniture Fair and is a video projection that reproduces views, both historical and current, of the Zona Tortona (a quadrilateral of streets in the southwest part of Milan). Initially the images appear fragmented, recomposing themselves at the touch of the viewer into a single photograph at full scale and full height (2.46 x 1.92 metres/8 x 6.3 feet). This opportunity has allowed the office to devise a new concept for shopfront windows. In fact, the company is currently working with National Geographic on a display window made of touchscreens embedded into the window via a metallic film and equipped with sensors that capture movement. The screens allow visitors to access video and information files about National Geographic from the street, blurring the threshold between interior and exterior. This type of application generates effects that go beyond the sensational qualities of corporate communication, opening up possible scenarios of interaction, modifying the perception of architectural spaces by their users, and demonstrating new applications not only in the realm of temporary installation design, but in the spaces of the everyday. Δ+

Translated from the Italian version into English by Paul David Blackmore

Valentina Croci is a freelance journalist of industrial design and architecture. She graduated from Venice University of Architecture (IUAV), and attained an MSc in architectural history from the Bartlett School of Architecture, London. She holds a PhD in industrial design sciences from the IUAV with a theoretical thesis on wearable digital technologies.

Text © 2007 John Wiley & Sons Ltd. Images: pp 150-51, 153 © dotdotdot srl; p 152 © dotdotdot srl, drawing Mauro Angelantoni

# Forming Climatic Change

The Architectural Association in London is renowned for its unique unit structure in which avant-garde research and design strategies are incubated and hatched. In a new series edited by Michael Weinstock, Academic Head at the AA, the activities of the units are brought under the spotlight. 'Unit Factor' kicks off with an account by **Steve Hardy** and **Werner Gaiser** of the Environments, Ecology and Sustainability research cluster they lead.

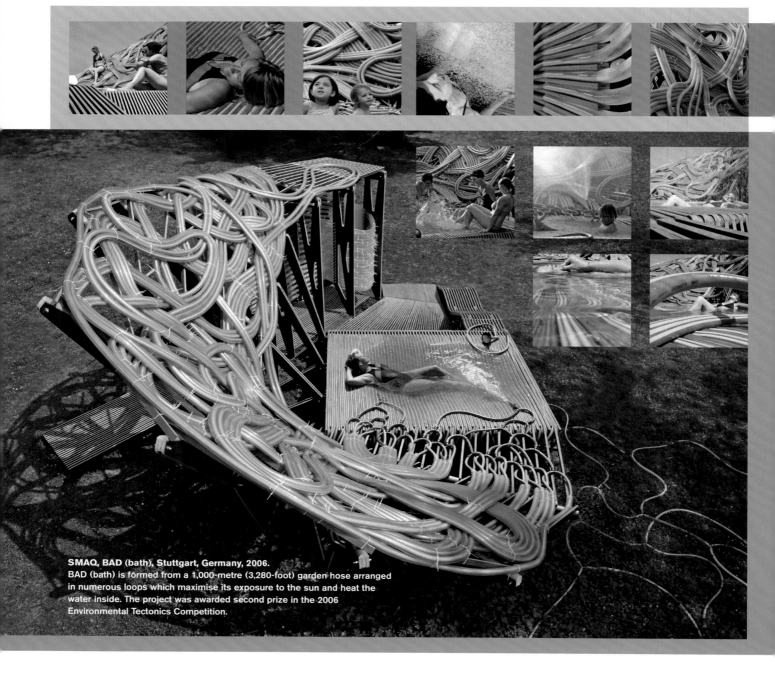

SMAQ, BAD (bath), Stuttgart, Germany, 2006.
BAD (bath) is formed from a 1,000-metre (3,280-foot) garden hose arranged in numerous loops which maximise its exposure to the sun and heat the water inside. The project was awarded second prize in the 2006 Environmental Tectonics Competition.

The widespread effects of climate change prompt a raised awareness in the general public and create a necessary preoccupation with environmental design that is rapidly transforming our society and design profession. In September 2006 a new platform was launched to discuss these challenges. The Environments, Ecology and Sustainability (EES) Research Cluster was formed by Brett Steele and Mike Weinstock of the Architectural Association with Steve Hardy and Werner Gaiser as its curators.

## Environmental Tectonics

Responding to the charge, the EES Research Cluster sponsored an international 'call for projects' competition – 'Environmental Tectonics'. The goal of the competition was to

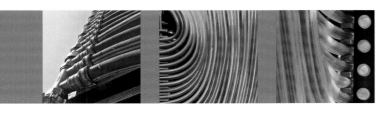

The array of loops heats water from 15°C heats to 47°C in less than two hours and provide, a leisure folly of aesthetic and experiential excess within the Solitude Palace Gardens near Stuttgart, Germany.

promote the potential of environmental design – conceptual, experimental or realised. The global response came from more than 20 countries and included a wide range of entries from students, researchers, practitioners, artists, scientists, engineers and architects.

The competition highlighted a plurality of approaches to environmental design and its associated tectonics. From this diversity, three main approaches emerged. Responding to environmental design as experiential design, a collection of projects investigated ephemeral effects in the subcategorical engagements of physiological phenomenology and material realism. Another set explored sustainable methods of construction examining low carbon processes while exploring vernacular or local resources. A third worked with performative or mitigatory structures and systems often with corresponding spatial effects.

One of the more novel approaches to the competition was BAD, a public bath located in the Solitude Palace Gardens near Stuttgart, Germany. Designed by Sabine Müller and Andreas Quednau of SMAQ, BAD (bath) explores the performative phenomenon of a warming garden hose taken to aesthetic and experiential extremes.

A 1,000-metre (3,280-foot) hose arranged in numerous loops maximises its exposure to the sun and heats the water inside. On an average day, water of approximately 15°C (59°F) heats to 47°C (116.6°F) in less than two hours. BAD (bath) takes environmental principles beyond pragmatic efficiencies and celebrates our typically hidden environmental systems.[1]

The competition work was clearly not *pro forma* – for the sake of form – but organisationally, spatially and materially formulated foremost from environmental parameters. From the 1960s a recombinant definition of environmental design shifted experiential approaches towards long-term temporalities formed from considering the needs of future generations. Strategies arose in terms of phasing, duration, processes of technique, temporal material effects and the long-term interaction of projects with natural flora and their environments.

## Extreme Environments

In addition to hosting the competition, the EES Research Cluster promotes other research initiatives. Steve Hardy and Jonas Lundberg initiated a design research project prompted by the United Nations resolution 'A/RES/58/214', which calls for the examination of vulnerable environments caused by climatic change. In contrast to low-carbon, high-efficiency structures, the research finds architectural potential in the mitigation of these extremes.

The ambition is to understand the reciprocal effects of the built environment on the complexity and performance of the natural ecosystem. Iterative design techniques continually re-form both the organisation itself and the context of which it is a part. Material and formal systems with simple rule-based conditions are explored, from which meta-systemic relationships emerge. The process yields projects that are not so much designed as grown and that, engaged within a temporal awareness, continue to evolve with the passing of time.

The Dune Stabiliser and Fog Harvester by Toby Burgess is a lightweight structure for use in the Namib Desert where fresh water is scarce due to recent aquifer depletion and consequential salination from the sea. A hydrophilic surface of Raschel mesh enables fog particles to coalesce and fall to the ground below. Nitinol, a shape memory alloy (SMA) muscle-wire filled with a super-absorbent polymer is capable of absorbing some of the captured moisture. In full saturation, the SMA muscle contracts by 17 per cent. Cumulative localised contractions continually optimise the global curvature of the surface towards the prevailing wind and fog.

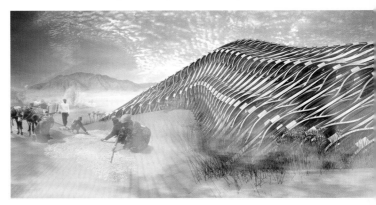

**Toby Burgess, Dune Stabiliser and Fog Harvester, Namib Desert, 2007**
The Dune Stabiliser is a lightweight deployable and adaptable structure with a dual layer of Raschel mesh that harvests the local fog into an irrigation system for the plants grown beneath its cover.

Toby Burgess, Dune Stabiliser and Fog Harvester, Namib Desert, 2007
A dual layer of Raschel mesh forms a hydrophilic surface, enabling minute fog particles to coalesce. The shape memory alloy muscle-wire is filled with a super-absorbent polymer allowing the muscle to contract and optimise the overall curvature of the structure.

The harvested water is used to nourish the flora beneath the canopy. Additionally, the mesh provides up to 70 per cent shade, modulating the sunlight and regulating the temperatures below. Flora, fertilised by the water, have a stabilising effect on the dune and over time the structure is moved to another location.[2] The growth spreads across the desert, creating a new and lasting landscape; the project operates within a short temporality projected along a longer-term evolutionary cycle.

In contrast to spans measured in years, 'contemporary design techniques are themselves temporal process driven methods'.[3] Iterative design processes explore evolutionary formation strategies that work with complex variables from natural phenomena and local contexts. These processes, as in Tom Tong's project described below, focus on the growth of seminatural systems, qualitative complexities and meta-systemic variations.

Tong's Pyroclastic Decomposé is situated around Naples within the uncontrolled, illegal developments around Vesuvius. Its regenerative and mitigative strategy is aimed at protecting the UNESCO World Heritage Sites further down the mountainside. The project integrates infrastructural topographies with sacrificial towers distributed by a non-linear tessellation system.

Vesuvius' main volcanic hazard is from a pyroclastic flow of gases and solids 'flowing' up to 150 kilometres (93 miles) an hour with temperatures of 1,000°C (1,832°F).[4] Uncontrolled urbanisation[5] has produced an increase in population and growing slum settlements, greatly increasing perceived vulnerabilities.[6] A Voronoi tessellation organises the surrounding landscape and helps dissipate the intensity of the pyroclastic flow. Topographical mounds reduce the flowing solids while the porous towers assist the upper dissipation of gases. In combination, these lower the speed, absorb the energy and reduce the temperature, making the flow less likely to reach the historic city.[7]

Together with the National Institute of Geology and Volcanology in Pisa, digital simulations were developed to optimise the system's performance. Variations of porosity, orientation, density and size occur as modifications within the field. Fully quantifiable optimisations are not applicable as the complexity of the pyroclastic phenomenon operates within innumerable probabilities and contingencies. Instead the magnitude of the situation requires one to look for qualitative shifts. By mitigating these indeterminate probabilities, the project hopes to protect the present occupation of a historic city from potential future events.

**Environmental Contingencies**
A definitive understanding of environmental design, often associated with low-carbon and performative efficiency, has yet to fully exist. Promises of new tectonics come from cultural changes in long-sighted temporalities arising from the recombinant definition of environmental and sustainable design.

Designs focused on carbon footprints and fixed performances are continually challenged by the changing fluidities of inhabitation and context. As the environment continues to evolve, we and our buildings will exist in radically different environments tomorrow. Performances optimised to specific situations may cease to function in new environments. The contingencies of change suggest that we design for semipredictable, composite situations and

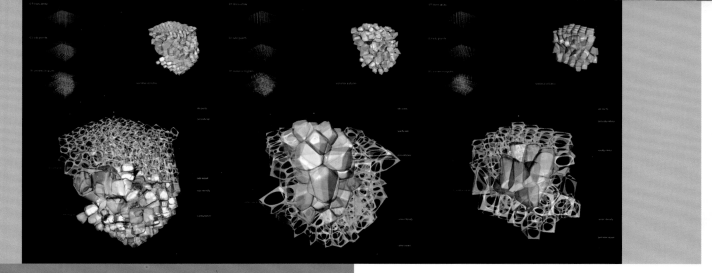

Tom Tong, Pyroclastic Decomposé, Naples, Italy, 2007
An iterative script is used to 'grow' the variations of Voronoi density and specify either structural voids, solids or conglomerates. The systemic variations are tested in flow simulations for optimised disruption behaviours.

performances. A composite or co-possible system needs to perform against consistent heat gain at present and torrential rainfall in the future. Associating these different potentials produces indeterminacies impossible to fully resolve in a single component or tectonic organisation.

Continual probing will inevitably locate architecture and environmental design research opting to perform in unstable and developing environments. Undoubtedly these will require different systemic and evolutionary logics able to cope with future contingencies and ecologies. The new material organisations will need to cope with multiple variables of form, space and performance distributed not only in space, but also within an emerging temporal perspective. ∆+

Steve Hardy is a member of Urban Future Organization, an international architecture office and design research collaborative. The office has won a number of international competitions, has exhibited its work at the Venice Biennale and Beijing Biennale and was recently featured in *10 X10 v. 2.* Hardy is co-unit master of Dip16 at the Architectural Association where he is also co-curator for EES Research.

Werner Gaiser has worked with Atelier Brückner and with the Design Partnership in San Francisco as project designer, and in 2003 joined BDSP Partnership. He is currently teaching sustainable and environmental design at the Architectural Association where he is co-curator for EES Research and is involved in the development of SUNtool, a tool for sustainable urban planning.

**Notes**
1. Sabine Müller and Andreas Quednau (SMAQ), 'Environmental Tectonics: A Call For Projects Competition 2006', BAD (bath), Architectural Association (London), 2006, p 1.
2. Toby Burgess, Dune Stabiliser and Fog Harvester, Dip16 2007, Fog Harvester Abstract, Architectural Association (London), 2007, p 1.
3. Ali Rahim, 'Potential performative effects', Architectural Design: Contemporary Techniques in Architecture, Wiley-Academy (Chichester), 2002, p 55.
4. Lucia Gurioli, R Cioni, A Sbrana and E Zanella, 'Sedimentology', Transport and Deposition of Pyroclastic Density Currents Over an Inhabited Area, Herculaneium (Rome), 2002, pp 49, 929–53.
5. Maria Luisa Carapezza, 'Vesuvius: 2000 Years of Observation', Civil Protection Agency (Rome), 2000, p 32.
6. Matteo Scaramella Abaton, 'UN-Habitat (2003) part IV: Summary of City Case Studies', Global Report on Human Settlements 2003: The Challenge of Slums, Earthscan (London), 2003, pp 195–228.
7. Tom Tong, Pyroclastic Decomposé, Dip16 2007, Pyroclastic Decomposé Abstract, Architectural Association (London), 2007, p 2.

Text © 2007 John Wiley & Sons Ltd. Images: p 154 © SMAQ, photos W Sulzbach, H Betwieser and SMAQ; pp 155-56 © Toby Burgess; p 157 © Chun Chung Thomas Tong

A Voronoi decomposition is used to organise a semiporous sacrificial tower in suburban Naples. The towers are variably distributed and together with a new landscape create a mitigation proposal to protect the UNESCO World Heritage City from the intensity of possible pyroclastic flow.

# Gods Are in the Details
# The Ambika Temple at Jagat

**Adam Hardy** is the author of a significant new book, *The Temple Architecture of India*. Here he describes the Ambika Temple at Jagat in Rajasthan, and suggests the lessons that contemporary architects might learn from this ancient structure.

The Ambika Temple, Jagat, from the south. A porch leads to the *mandapa*, audience hall of the enshrined deity, leading via an antechamber to the dark sanctum beneath the tower. Above the antechamber, divine power is radiated from the front of the tower through a cascade of pullulating horseshoe arch dormer motifs (*gavakshas*).

It is common among the traditions of Indian temple architecture to find that successively more complex designs have been extrapolated from the earlier ones. Through this process the temple architects achieve a mesmerising sense of movement, though often at the expense of tactile presence. Certain works occupy a happy cusp between sensuous plasticity and sensational proliferation. The small temple at Jagat (c AD 961), near Udaipur in Rajasthan, dedicated to the goddess Ambika, stands at such a moment in the development of the Nagara (north Indian) tradition, when the single-spired Latina shrine form had only lately burgeoned out of itself into the composite Shekhari mode, with its unfurling conglomeration of interpenetrating shrine-images.

The temple is raised on a continuously stepped pedestal, carrying the moulded base that follows the undulations of the wall. This wall, with its goddess icons (in the cardinal niches), its guardian deities of the eight directions (on the corners), its heavenly company of angels, minstrels and curvaceous nymphs and its horned lions twisting in the shadows, is understandably the usual focus for art historians. But to see the wall as a sculptural frieze, as they tend to, is to decapitate the temple and miss the aedicular structure underlying the architectural composition.

Indian temples are composed of a multiplicity of what, in our age of fractal geometry, may be called self-similar forms. These are aedicules or images of shrines, microcosms of the temple as a whole. Just as a god may have many manifestations, a temple design is conceived as containing numerous smaller temples, embedded within the whole or within one another, emerging and expanding downwards and outwards. The aedicular elements of the Ambika Temple are of two types: one with a curved spire (*shikhara*), like the large one at the core of the tower; the other with a tiered pyramidal roof, like the large one crowning the hall. As these forms derive from an imagery of thatched roofs, integral to both types of aedicule is the horseshoe arch dormer window motif, which multiplies and fragments in stepped cascades that surge down the layered eaves. Neither the spirelets nor the miniature halls should be looked at in isolation from the corresponding wall projections, which are conceived as pillars, made explicit by their capitals. Each of these embedded pillars, together with its crown, forms an aedicular component termed a *kuta-stambha* ('pavilion-topped pillar'). Diagram c opposite shows the type with the diminutive spire.

On the cardinal axes a cluster of elements creates the image of a known shrine type (Diagram d) emerging from the chest of the temple tower. This idea, though perennial in Indian temple architecture, is not unique to it. After all, the Romans, housing all the gods in their Pantheon at a more monumental scale (45 metres/148 feet high compared with 10 metres/33 feet), placed one temple form on the front of another. But where, as at Jagat, all is multi-aedicular, the projected form looms subtly from the matrix.

The hall has its own axial clusters to complete the centrifugal swell. Inside, it is the main ceiling bay (Diagram b opposite) that provides a corresponding sense of downward and outward growth. Unlike the lacy corbelled ceilings of a century later, this one is just 2 metres (6.5 feet) across and scooped out of a couple of abutted slabs. Not exactly Pantheonesque in size or construction, it is nonetheless more cosmic in its expansion than the mightiest of domes. It blossoms down through proliferating, ribbed dome-images (equivalent to the exterior shrine-images), through an unfolding, progressively emanating geometry of circles and squares.